DOING RESEARCH IN FASHION AND DRESS

DOING RESEARCH IN FASHION AND DRESS

An Introduction to Qualitative Methods

Yuniya Kawamura

Bloomsbury Academic
An imprint of Bloomsbury Publishing Plc

BLOOMSBURY
LONDON · OXFORD · NEW YORK · NEW DELHI · SYDNEY

Bloomsbury Academic

An imprint of Bloomsbury Publishing Plc

50 Bedford Square
London
WC1B 3DP
UK

1385 Broadway
New York
NY 10018
USA

www.bloomsbury.com

Bloomsbury is a registered trade mark of Bloomsbury Publishing Plc

English edition first published in 2011 by Berg
Reprinted by Bloomsbury Academic 2013, 2015

British Library Cataloguing-in-Publication Data
A catalogue record for this book is available from the British Library.

ISBN: HB: 978-1-8478-8583-8
PB: 978-1-8478-8582-1
ePUB: 978-1-8478-8734-4

Library of Congress Cataloging-in-Publication Data
A catalog record for this book is available from the Library of Congress.

Typeset by Apex Publishing, LLC, Madison, WI

To My Family

CONTENTS

ACKNOWLEDGMENTS

I thank the Fashion Institute of Technology (FIT)/State University of New York for granting me a sabbatical leave during the Spring 2010 semester to work on my research projects, one of which was the completion of this book. Parts of the book were presented at various sociology and fashion/dress studies conferences, and my trips to these conferences were partially funded by the Teaching Institute at FIT's Center for Excellence in Teaching (CET).

I am always grateful to Valerie Steele, Director of the Museum at FIT, and Joanne Eicher, Regents' Professor Emerita of the University of Minnesota, who set the high standards in fashion/dress studies. They have been my inspirational role models and mentors.

My appreciation also goes to all my colleagues in the Social Sciences Department at FIT, Yasemin Celik, Paul Clement, Luis Zaera, Ernest Poole, Spencer Schein, Meg Miele, Joseph Maiorca, Roberta Paley, Praveen Chaudhry, Emre Ozsoz, Dan Benkendorf, Jung-Whan (Marc) de Jong, and Beatrice Farkas, who are always supportive of my work and whose friendship I cherish. Students in my "Clothing and Society" and "Cultural Expressions of Non-Western Dress/Fashion" classes provided a valuable sounding board for the development of my ideas. I share their enthusiasm and passion for fashion.

I am also thankful to Professor Hiroshi Ishida, his colleagues and his staff at the Social Science Institute at the University of Tokyo in Japan, with which I was affiliated as a Visiting Fellow during my sabbatical, for providing me with research facilities on campus to work on this project, and thanks also to my old classmates from Columbia University, Tsutomu (Tom) Nakano of Aoyama Gakuin University and Takeshi Wada of Tokyo University whose friendship and collegiality I very much appreciated while I was finishing this book in Tokyo.

Every time I publish a book, I look back at my days at the Nihon Keizai Shimbun (Nikkei) in New York. The staff there gave me the opportunity to write articles about the fashion industry in New York in their publications as a correspondent, and that eventually led me to graduate studies and to write my doctoral dissertation on fashion and sociology. Had they not given me that opportunity, I would have never been inspired to write about fashion and become a fashion scholar. I am who I am today because of my former colleagues at Nikkei, Tsuneo Kita (President and CEO of Nikkei, Inc.), Yuji Sonomoto (President of Nikkei Research, Inc.), Hisao Saida (Vice President of Nikkei Publishing, Inc.), Satoshi Okada, Yoshifumi Kimura, Masaki Morita, Norimichi Okai, and Susumu Kurata.

I feel very much honored to have been commissioned to write this book by Berg Publishers and Kathryn Earle, Managing Director. My gratitude also goes to Julia Hall, Senior Editor, who graciously agreed to extend the manuscript deadline and patiently waited for my manuscript to arrive. Thanks also go to Emily Medcalf, Sales and Marketing Executive, for helping me choose the right image as a cover of this book. This is the third book that I have published with Berg, and it is always a pleasure working with its efficient and professional editorial team.

I thank the gracious assistance provided by the library staff at the Fashion Institute of Technology, Columbia University, New York University, and the New York Public Library.

My appreciation also goes to my best friends Satoko Iye and Yutaka Ishibashi, whom I called and e-mailed frequently whenever I needed a distraction from writing. I have known them for more than twenty years, and their friendship is invaluable to me.

I dedicate this book to my family, Yoya, Yoko, and Maya Kawamura who constantly gave me words of encouragement during this project. They were always available with advice and assistance. I could not have completed this book without their love and support.

Yuniya Kawamura
New York/Tokyo

INTRODUCTION

Objectives

- To trace the history of fashion/dress studies.
- To distinguish fashion/dress—related debates, theories, and empirical studies.
- To learn when and how scholars, social scientists in particular, became interested in fashion/dress studies.
- To recognize the importance of defining terminologies and using culturally neutral terms.
- To examine ways to make fashion/dress studies a legitimate academic discipline.
- To explore an interdisciplinary approach to fashion/dress studies.
- To understand the overall contents of this book.

I write this book in the hope of making fashion/dress studies an established academic discipline as many fashion/dress scholars, including myself, have always insisted. It is common knowledge among scholars and research professionals (Kawamura 2005; Lipovetsky 1994; McRobbie 1998; Niessen and Brydon 1998; Palmer 1997; Ribeiro 1998; Taylor 2004) that fashion/dress[1] as a research topic in academia is often considered not serious enough and is treated as a marginal area of research, and thus, it does not deserve any intellectual considerations.

One of the reasons why fashion/dress is not taken as seriously as the scholars would like it to be is that there are no clearly articulated theoretical framework and methodological strategies to study fashion/dress. Nor do we recognize various methodological tools and options to investigate fashion/dress, especially when it is treated as an abstract concept rather than raw materials of clothing. We must make an attempt to make fashion/dress studies an established discipline that can stand on its own right and make it into an area of study that is similar to gender studies, cultural studies, or the media studies that transcends all disciplinary boundaries and includes interdisciplinary approaches that are appropriate for one's research goal.

Different writers had been interested in fashion and dress as early as the thirteenth century ever since the emergence of a fashion phenomenon in Europe, but the study of fashion/dress as an intellectual theme and a social scientific study that demands empiricism and objectivity is of recent origin. Before it became a legitimate research topic for scholars, social scientists in particular, it was the topic frequently discussed among philosophers and moralists who did not provide any empirical data or factual evidence. Still today, methods of research in fashion/dress studies have not yet been thoroughly explored in social science disciplines, such as sociology, psychology, and cultural anthropology, among others. There is hardly any literature specifically devoted to qualitative research methods in fashion/dress, except Lou Taylor's two informative books, *Establishing Dress History* (2004) and *The Study of Dress History* (2002), focusing on object-based research in the history of fashion and dress. More recently, Flynn and Foster's book entitled *Research Methods for the Fashion Industry* (2009) was published primarily for fashion industry professionals and practitioners. Many scholars as well as students are reluctant to pick fashion/dress as their research topic because of the lack of information or literature on methodological strategies, and this book attempts to fill that void; by doing so, I hope to give fashion/dress studies the value and respect it deserves in the world of academia in addition to providing practical procedures and processes of research. We see a growing number of textbooks and literature on qualitative research methods in social sciences in general, but few are written particularly for academic fashion/dress studies.

For us to conduct research, we need to do it empirically, scholarly, and scientifically. This book is not meant for practitioners in fashion business, but it could be used by anyone who wants to study fashion/dress empirically and objectively using qualitative research methods. The methods I elaborate in this book are by no means exhaustive but can be treated as the primary qualitative methodological tools found in fashion/dress studies. Some researchers only believe that research is considered a research when the methodology is quantitative and not qualitative, but as indicated in subsequent chapters in this book, there are descriptive data that can be retrieved only by qualitative strategies.

Therefore, this book provides students with a guided introduction to qualitative research methods, and the aim is to do this through a mix of theoretical and practical perspectives, offering contextual material on fashion/dress–related studies and also how-to accounts of best practice. It offers step-by-step instructions on how to go about applying particular methods in practice and suggestions on what can be neglected or not neglected in the research process as well as the strengths and the weaknesses of each method. In order for students to understand what it takes to research fashion/dress, we need to refer to significant fashion- and dress-related studies in which the authors indicate their methods. I have intentionally selected the studies as examples in which the researchers' methodologies are explained clearly and in detail as well as the ones that focus on Western and non-Western fashion and dress.

THE HISTORY OF FASHION/DRESS STUDIES

Individuals, rich or poor, young or old, men or women, have always been interested in fashion or how people dressed at one point in time. Even before the emergence of social sciences, writers picked fashion/dress as a topic in various publications, such as books, newspapers, journals, and so forth. I trace the historical development of interests in fashion and fashion/dress studies to address the contributions of diverse areas of knowledge and to examine how the questions that it has addressed have shifted from simple commentaries, descriptive essays, and anecdotes on fashion/dress to empirical scientific research.

The history of fashion/dress studies can be classified into three stages and time periods: (1) interests in and debates about fashion/dress as discussion topics, (2) scholarly writings on fashion/dress discourse and theories, and (3) empirical fashion/dress studies in social sciences with the indication of specific methodological approaches.

INTERESTS IN AND DEBATES ABOUT FASHION/DRESS AS A DISCUSSION TOPIC

While many fashion researchers believe that fashion as a topic is a recent one, it has been of long interest to many classical writers and novelists. According to Johnson, Torntore, and Eicher (2003: 1), the study of fashion and dress has been and still is widely conducted by individuals reflecting many disciplines, and they argue that interest in fashion is not a recent one.[2] They take us back to 1575 when Michel de Montaigne, one of the earliest writers of dress, questions why human begins to wear clothes in the first place. Interest in fashion/dress obviously parallels with the fashion phenomenon that first began in Italy and then moved to France (Laver 1995 [1969]; Lipovetsky 1994; Perrot 1994; Steele 1988). Numerous accounts on fashion/dress are found in the historical archives and literature.

For example, Charles de Secondat Montesquieu (1689–1755), a French social critic and a political thinker, in *Persian Letters* (1973 [1721]), writes about the rapid changes in fashion in Paris (Letter No. 99): "A woman who leaves Paris to spend six months in the country comes back looking antiquated as if she had been away for thirty years. A son will fail to recognize a portrait of his mother because the dress in which she had been painted seems so alien." In 1831, Thomas Carlyle, an English philosopher, explains the functions of clothing/fashion and says that the first purpose of clothes was not for warmth or modesty but adornment, which is believed to be a universal practice.

While some writers did not appreciate fashion and condemned it, many French novelists and philosophers discussed fashion in their writings. Jean-Jacques Rousseau (1712–1780), an advocate of simple living and an opponent of luxury and fashion, in his *Discours sur les sciences et les arts* (1997 [1750]), writes that fashion destroyed virtue and masked vice, and fashion has a negative impact on people's morals. On the other hand, French writers and poets, such as Honoré de Balzac (1799–1850) and Charles Baudelaire (1821–1867), were in support of fashion and wrote about it favorably (Kawamura 2004). Whether the writers thought fashion was moral or immoral, frivolous or not frivolous, it is important to note that they still paid much attention to the phenomenon of fashion. However, these writings do not offer any theoretical framework or implications, and we only see that there were fashion phenomena and interests in as well as a commotion over fashion.

ACADEMIC INTERESTS IN FASHION/DRESS DISCOURSE AND THEORIES

Scholars' interests in fashion/dress as a legitimate research topic began to emerge as fashion changes were taking place more and more rapidly during and after the Industrial Revolution in the latter half of the nineteenth century. The social structure of the Western world underwent a great transformation in the eighteenth and nineteenth centuries. The population increased, productivity soared, and a money economy developed that resulted in the expansion of commerce, improved technology, and the possibility of social mobility. The invention of the sewing machine made it possible to manufacture, in large quantities at cheaper prices, fashionable clothes that used to be handmade and were, therefore, time-consuming and expensive. As fashion became increasingly democratized and widespread throughout Europe, it attracted a great deal of attention from the masses, and at the same time, it changed people's views as well as scholars' perspectives on fashion/dress. Dress history publications, such as those by Quicherat (1877) and Racinet (1888), began to appear in France.

When social and behavioral sciences were becoming established as a discipline at the turn of the twentieth century, one of the first questions that interested anthropologists and psychologists was "Why do people wear clothes?" Many theoretical explanations were developed to address this basic question. For instance, Hiler (1930: 1–12) raised the following theories: the economic theory, the theory of possession, the theory of sex attraction, totemistic theories, and the theory of amulets to explain the origin of clothing. Others (Brenninkmeyer 1963: 14–47; Kaiser 1998: 15–17) may have used different terms, such as the modesty/immodesty theory, adornment/decoration theory, and protection theory, but they overlap with Hiler's in their contents in explaining the origin of fashion, not clothing.

Some of the scholars toward the end of the nineteenth century and the beginning of the twentieth century laid the solid foundation of classical theories of fashion.[3] For Simmel (1957 [1904]) and Veblen (1957 [1899]), fashion is used to differentiate oneself from others; it includes a group that wears a similar style and excludes others who do not dress like the group. Class inclusion and exclusion are the opposite sides of the same coin. Sumner (1940 [1906]) and Toennies (1961 [1909]) looked at a fashion phenomenon as the decline in social customs. Social customs dictate and determine how we are supposed to dress in which there is little room for fashion creativity and aesthetic expression. In contrast, as social customs begin to weaken, fashion begins to prosper, and people begin to desire social distinction. That is the beginning of fashion. Tarde (1903) looks at a cycle of fashion as innovation, imitation, and opposition. When something is innovated, it is imitated in order for it to be disseminated, and then once it is imitated, a new thing is again innovated. It is in a constant cycle. Several classical scholars' take on fashion is primarily based on the trickle-down theory of fashion, that is, imitation (Simmel 1957 [1904]; Sumner 1940 [1906]; Tarde 1903; Toennies 1961 [1909]; Veblen 1957 [1899]). One thing that is clearly stated is that their focus is not dress or clothing but fashion. They treat fashion synonymously with the concept of imitation. It takes two to imitate or imitation to occur: the imitator and the imitated. There is a social relationship between the two. The emphasis among the scholars may differ, but they all agree that fashion is a social process of imitation.

Furthermore, these studies are not empirical, but the classical theorists made an important contribution to the studies of fashion/dress, which is always used as a departing point of discussion.[4] Fashion/dress researchers began to slowly move away from object-based research in which the focus was solely on tangible clothing items (Taylor 2004). These classical scholars theorized and conceptualized the notion of fashion, and they explored the sociological significance and meaning of fashion in their unique perspectives. It helps us understand what fashion meant toward the end of the nineteenth century. Then we can begin to compare the contemporary understanding of fashion with the classical interpretation of fashion. Based on their theories, we can examine how fashion changes and evolves, and that may help us conduct various empirical studies and construct a new theory or theories of fashion to explicate today's fashion.

EMPIRICAL FASHION/DRESS STUDIES IN SOCIAL SCIENCES

While the classical studies of fashion were often theoretical and discourse-oriented, fashion/dress studies in the twentieth century became increasingly empirical. There is a shift from theoretical assumptions to empirical studies with various methodological inquiries. Many scholars agree that Western societies went through a transition in the past several decades, and people's patterns of consumption changed visibly. Consumers' tastes and preferences were becoming increasingly diverse, and so is fashion. It used to be rather easy to find fashion's source and define it. But as the new structure of society began to form and with the advent of technology, fashion information spread from various locations through multiple media sources at an amazingly fast pace not only vertically but also horizontally. Fashion can no longer be explained merely by the concept of imitation or the trickle-down theory as indicated earlier.

According to Roach-Higgins and Eicher (1973: 26–7), social scientists have begun to take interest in dress and fashion only recently. In the late 1920s and the 1930s, there was an upsurge of interest in publications on the psychological, social, and cultural implications of dress, and this interest no doubt was associated with general sharp breaks with tradition at that time, symbolized so well in the dress of women (Roach-Higgins and Eicher 1973: 29–30). Therefore, since the majority of social science research is empirical, fashion research also became empirical requiring the researchers to have solid, scientific methodological strategies. Without methods, there is no empiricism, and without empiricism, there is no social scientific research on fashion/dress.

In 1919, Kroeber measured the illustrations of women's dress in fashion plates that were idealized depictions of women's clothing styles. This is one of the rare and earlier studies of fashion/dress using a quantitative method. In 1922, Radcliffe-Brown conducted a fieldwork study of the Andaman Islanders near the Bay of Bengal in India and explored the relationship between people and ornament/amulets that are used to dress and decorate human bodies. Personal ornament serves two functions, desires for protection and for display. In 1924, Bogardus examined the meaning of a fad and published an article in the *Journal of Applied Sociology*; his study was based on ten-year research. In 1930, Hiler published his work, which was based on one thousand collected references to clothing and ornament from numerous disciplines.

In the late 1930s, Young conducted a statistical analysis of fashion trends (1937), and she found that there are fixed and predictable patterns. She reviewed historical evidence in fashion plates and magazines. According to Young (1937), there are three defined recurring cycles in skirt silhouettes every thirty-eight to forty years. Thus, fashion trends are repeated. Harni takes a case-study approach in his empirical research and explores fetishism, transvestism, and tattooing (1932).

Fashion/dress scholars in the 1940s and 1950s began to look at the social and psychological aspects of clothing. In the 1960s, studies in fashion/dress became more sophisticated and deeply empirical (Horn 1968; Ryan 1966). About fifty years after the first psychological interest in clothing emerged, in 1965, Rosencranz looked at numerous motives related to clothing that were often disguised and were complex even for a single situation (Kaiser 1998: 23). Psychologists and social psychologists began to consider the potential of clothing as a variable to be manipulated in experiments, and in the 1960s, a distinction between "hippies" and "straight" attire prompted an interest as perceived by other people. Theories dealing with how people form impressions about other people were developed under the rubric of a cognitive perspective, focusing on how people simplify their perceptions and develop judgments about other people on the basis of certain cues (Kaiser 1998: 24).

Blumer is one of the earliest scholars who rejected the imitation theory or the class differentiation model of fashion proposed by the classical theorists of fashion, such as Simmel, Veblen, Spencer, and Tarde among others. Blumer conducted an ethnographical study in Paris (1969a), and he came to the conclusion that the imitation theory may be valid in explaining fashion in the sixteenth, seventeenth, or eighteenth century but not contemporary fashion. He interviewed designers, buyers, and other fashion professionals working in Paris fashion and argued that fashion no longer comes from the top and trickles down to the masses. Fashion is a collective activity and is a collective taste. The job of a designer is to accurately predict what the collective taste is going to be the next season. Many contemporary writers who followed Blumer, such as Davis (1992) and Crane (2000), also negate the imitation theory of fashion.

Contemporary fashion/dress studies needs to be extremely empirical while articulating clearly which methodologies are used and how the research is conducted. Furthermore, they should not be distracted by fashion magazines or fashion-related information on the Internet, which lack objectivity, the very essence of social sciences. Fashion and fashion information have become easily accessible to almost anyone, and therefore, data that can be used in fashion/dress research must be collected carefully and with much caution.

THE USE OF TERMINOLOGIES

As we review and analyze various empirical studies on fashion/dress, each with specific research methodologies, we need to be aware of the definitions of these terms, such as fashion, dress, clothes, costume, and so forth. Different writers use different definitions of the variables relating to the topic being reviewed. The differences may need to be taken into consideration in a research process of the literature review, which is described in Chapter 2, "Research Process." In studying fashion/dress, many researchers often use "fashion," "dress," and "clothes/clothing" interchangeably while others make an attempt to separate these concepts clearly. It is important to clarify the definitions and how they are used because writers and researchers have different meanings of words.

Kaiser gives clear definitions of the terms that are often used in fashion/dress studies, such as adornment, apparel, appearance, clothing, costume, dress, fashion, style, and wearable art (1998: 4–5). It is also true, as Kaiser convincingly points out, that each discipline with its own approach and perspective to fashion and dress may have its own definition of each term, and that needs to be clarified in the beginning of research (Kaiser 1998: 3) because some may be culturally specific or gender-specific. While it is difficult to maintain the neutral standpoint in creating a definition, having the awareness is the key to conducting an objective, bias-free research.

First, we need to examine whether the writer is talking about fashion as a distinct concept that stands out from other relevant concepts, such as dress, apparel, costume, or garb, or he is treating it as a synonym of these words loosely tied to fashion. Some scholars may even choose not to use the term "fashion," realizing that it is the term that has specific meanings. Second, it must be made clear to the readers that the term "dress" does not mean a dress worn only by women as used in our everyday language. As Kaiser explains:

> Distinctions need to be clarified between everyday usage of clothing-related terms and conceptual usage of the same words, as we attempt to study cloth- ing and human behavior. At times, confusion may be created by the connota- tions words have for us in everyday life as contrasted with their conceptual definitions. Furthermore, for example, the word dress may conjure an image of a female's article of clothing, whereas clothing scholars use the term to refer to a more generic idea. (Kaiser 1998: 3–4)

For those who study dress from an academic point of view, dress can include body modifications, such as scarification and tattooing as well as sartorial covering (John- son, Torntore, and Eicher 2003: 1).

FASHION

According to Baudrillard (1972), "fashion" is one of the most inexplicable phenom- ena. Edward Sapir (1931: 139) also explains that the meaning of the term "fashion" may be clarified by pointing out how it differs in connotation from a number of other terms whose meaning it approaches.

When a word appears in a dictionary, it is plausible evidence that the word is used widely in the society. Etymologists and historical linguists say that it was prob- ably about the year 1300 that a sense of style, fashion, or manner of dress was first recorded. *The Dictionnaire de la mode au XXe siècle* (Remaury 1996) indicates more specifically that the French word for fashion "mode," which meant the collective manner of dressing, first appeared in 1482. Clearly, there was a fashion phenomenon at that time. The word "mode" originally comes from the Latin word *modus*, which means manner in English or *manière* in French. By the end of the fifteenth century, fashion had the meaning of a current usage, or a conventional usage in dress or life- style especially as observed in upper circles of society. The English word "fashion" comes originally from the Latin word *facio* or *factio*, which means making or doing (Barnard 1996; Brenninkmeyer 1963: 2). According to Brenninkmeyer (1963: 2), the predominant social notion of fashion arose early in the sixteenth century via the sense of a special manner of making clothes.

There are conflicting views as to when fashion was born. Heller explains:

> Scholars, particularly in art and costume history, have argued and accepted that fashion was not really born before around 1350. Those who are familiar with the Old French literature of the twelfth and thirteenth centuries may find that astonishing, since very concise descriptions of fashionable clothing abound in that corpus. (Heller 2007: 1)

The examples of fashion in noble male characters in thirteenth-century literature are numerous, and men were at the forefront of consumption and display through the Middle Ages (Heller 2007: 4).

Fashion exists in many areas of life, not only in the way we dress, but also in many other areas such as food, home furnishings, and even our ways of thinking. Most often, however, dress becomes the focus when fashion arises as a topic of discussion. Fashion often represents clothing-fashion, that is, the most trendy, up-to-date clothing that the majority of the people in society adopts and follows. Fashion does encompass more than clothing, but the studies that I refer to in this book mostly talk about clothing-fashion and other items related to clothing such as accessories and adornment.

The term "fashion" is an elusive term, and thus it is not easy to define. Many treat it as clothing-fashion and use the terms "clothing" and "fashion" interchangeably as if they are synonyms. But those who feel passionate about fashion and those who wish to pursue careers in the fashion industry would argue that the term "fashion" stands out. If someone says "You are wearing fashion today," the statement carries a specific implication and message. It is different from "You are wearing clothes today." The reactions and responses to these comments are different. Therefore, it is quite apparent that the social meaning and interpretation of the word "fashion" is exclusive and socially meaningful.

While there are studies that pinpoint the word "fashion" and explore how that word and phenomenon came about, there are others that are simply talking about dress or clothes and occasionally use the term "fashion." The studies in this book used as examples include both types, that is, fashion and dress, and therefore, I use them side by side. While understanding the exact meaning and definition of "fashion" is important as part of an intellectual discussion/debate and the word itself fascinates us, it is not the goal of this book to investigate them.

CULTURALLY NEUTRAL TERMS: AVOIDING EUROCENTRISM/ETHNOCENTRISM

Words carry implications and connotations that may already be imbued with ethnocentrism and biases, and in order to avoid ethnocentrism and prejudices, scholars suggest using terms such as body supplements and body modifications, instead of terms such as veils, which have culturally specific implications, according to Eicher and Roach-Higgins (1992: 1–28), and they go further to find the most appropriate term to describe non-Western clothes. The term "non-Western" already has biases implying that it is not Western while using the West as the standard. Terms such as "peasant dress" or "folk dress" also do not sound appropriate. The most neutral term that is used is "ethnic dress," which implies that one belongs to an ethnic group in which values, norms, traditions, and beliefs among many other characteristics are shared.

Eicher, Evenson, and Lutz propose a specific classification system of dress and come up with their own definition of dress. They explain (Eicher et al. 2008: 4): "Our definition of dress as body modifications and body supplements includes more than clothing, or even clothing and accessories. Our definition encompasses many ways of dressing ourselves. In addition to covering our bodies, we apply color to our skins by use of cosmetics, whether paints or powders, and also apply color and pattern through tattoos." They also include adding scent, modifying taste, and making sound as part of "dress." Wearers and observers perceive characteristics of any individual's total dress through all five senses, such as sight, touch, smell, sound, and taste. They explain that body modifications are the alterations of the body itself that relate to all of these five senses while body supplements are the items that are placed upon the body, most often thought of as garments by Euro-Americans (Eicher et al. 2008: 6).

The advantages of this classification system are: (1) It reduces the likelihood of using words that are inherently biased or imply cultural superiority, as is often the case in any indigenous language; (2) It provides the understanding of the details of the physical forms of dress items and practices and the relationship of this form to the body. Culturally specific terms subsume this information and can lead to misconceptions when applied cross-culturally; (3) Culturally specific terms for dress items and processes also assume a social context of use for each aspect of dress; and (4) It highlights the relationship between the complexity and detail apparent in any dress ensemble and the role of those elements of dress in nonverbal communication about the identity, activity, and particular mood of the wearer (Eicher et al. 2008: 25–8).

MAKING FASHION/DRESS STUDIES A LEGITIMATE ACADEMIC DISCIPLINE

In the nineteenth century, social sciences were still in their infancy. The academic world was not yet divided into specialized departments. For instance, we now know Herbert Spencer (1820–1903) as an American sociologist, but he wrote about biology, philosophy, economics, and sociology while Karl Marx (1818–1883), a German political scientist, wrote about philosophy, economics, law, and politics, among many other topics. Academic disciplines began to differentiate over the course of the nineteenth century and different academic disciplines in the field of social sciences were born. That led to different departments in colleges and universities, and the boundaries among disciplines became clearer.

ACADEMIC DEVALUATION

Studies of fashion/dress in social sciences include anthropology, economics, history, political science, psychology, sociology, communication studies, cultural studies, media studies, and feminist studies, among others. Up until the 1990s, scholars often mentioned the academic devaluation of fashion/dress as a topic. Niessen and Brydon (1998: ix–x) wrote: "Fashion and clothing have for a long while remained scholarly unmentionables." According to Niessen and Brydon (1998: x–xi), in the 1950s and 1960s, diverse writers were slowly able to give theoretical weight to those people who understand their own thoughts and actions in relation to body decoration. Similarly, Taylor (2002a: 1) writes: "[F]our hundred years of development of dress history in Europe and the United States have taken place outside the boundaries of 'academic respectability' and the residues of this prejudice remain a debated issue." McRobbie (1998: 15) makes an attempt to argue against the lower academic status of fashion/dress studies and writes: "[This] is based upon the assumption that fashion, despite its trivialized status, is a subject worthy of study." Lipovetsky also argues:

> [T]he question of fashion is not a fashionable one among intellectuals... Fashion is celebrated in museums, but among serious intellectual preoccupations it has marginal status. It turns up everywhere on the street, in industry, and in the media, but it has virtually no place in the theoretical inquiries of our thinkers. Seen as an ontologically and socially inferior domain, it is unproblematic and undeserving of investigation; seen as a superficial issue, it discourages conceptual approaches. (Lipovetsky 1994: 3–4)

In order for us to create fashion/dress studies as a discipline, we need to define the studies and explain what the studies encompass. For instance, Kaiser defines the social psychology of clothing as follows:

> The social psychology of clothing is concerned with the various means people use to modify the appearance of the body, as well as the social and psychological forces that lead to, and result from, processes of managing personal appearance. Fashion/dress scholars should not simply look at clothing as concrete, visible and material items but treat it in a more abstract sense. (Kaiser 1998: 4)

I also proposed a new discipline called "fashion-ology" in my *Fashion-ology: An Introduction to Fashion Studies* (2005), which is another name for a sociology of fashion. Fashion studies may include studies on dress, apparel, clothes, accessories, shoes, and cosmetics. I introduce a specific theoretical framework, which is exactly the study of the concept, the idea, or the phenomenon of "fashion." I clearly state that "It is neither the study of dress nor the study of clothing, which means that the two, fashion and dress/clothing, are different concepts and entities which can be or should be studied separately" (Kawamura 2005: 1). I define fashion-ology as a sociological investigation of fashion, and it treats fashion as a system of institutions that produces the concept as well as the phenomenon/practice of fashion (Kawamura 2005: 1). Not all sociological investigations of fashion look at institutional factors like mine does, but my primary focus is the social nature of fashion in its production, distribution, diffusion, reception, adoption, and consumption. My theory of fashion-ology is backed by my fieldwork study on famous Japanese designers who became successful in Paris fashion in the 1970s and 1980s (Kawamura 2004), which is discussed further in Chapter 4, "Survey Methods." While not all fashion scholars make it that explicit, there are those who imply that it is fashion that they are focusing on and not clothing or dress.

Fashion or dress as a research topic is still definitely not in the mainstream academic arena even in the twenty-first century. Fashion/dress scholars need to think of strategies and ways to elevate the academic status of fashion. One of the reasons why it is often taken lightly is, as indicated earlier, the lack of the methodological inquiry in fashion/dress studies. Thus in this book, I propose and explore several methodological strategies so that fashion/dress can be brought into the same terrain as other scholarly fields, particularly in social sciences.

MAKING FASHION/DRESS STUDIES INTERDISCIPLINARY

Disciplines are often territorial, and scholars tend to exclude those in other disciplines, which creates a serious and an unpleasant rift among different fields of research, and this must be avoided. For example, O'Connor explains:

> [C]ultural studies and sociology have sought to exclude anthropologists from the study of fashion through the use of a simplistic modernity paradigm that goes as follows: Western fashion changes and is modern. Non-Western clothing is fixed, traditional and does not change. Therefore, it is asserted, anthropologists can have nothing to say about modern Western fashion. (O'Connor 2005: 41)

However, such ways of thinking are now replaced with a new idea that supports interdisciplinary endeavors. A number of academic disciplines in the social sciences and humanities have contributed to our understanding and analysis of clothing and human behavior. For example, there are significant anthropological fashion/dress studies, such as Hansen's (2000) study on secondhand clothing consumption as a Zambian cultural economy of taste and style.

Therefore, we can regard fashion/dress studies as an interdisciplinary area of knowledge that has emerged because of theories and research findings that cross traditional disciplinary boundaries, and it becomes possible to integrate and incorporate multiple, different methodological strategies. This will be discussed further in subsequent chapters.

Academic journals in fashion/dress studies began to emerge after the late 1960s, such as *Costume: Journal of the Costume Society of Great Britain* in 1967, *Dress: The Journal of the Costume Society of America* in 1975, and *Clothing and Textile Research Journal (CTRJ)* in 1982, which is the official publication of the International Textile and Apparel Association.

Although the progress may be gradual, toward the end of the twentieth century and into the twenty-first century, there are further optimistic changes in the field of fashion/dress studies. A groundbreaking journal called *Fashion Theory: The Journal of Dress, Body and Culture*, a peer-reviewed quarterly academic journal, was established in 1997 by Valerie Steele, a world-renowned fashion historian at the Fashion Institute of Technology in New York. It has research-based articles written by scholars in social sciences and humanities around the world. The journal helped raise the level of the topic in academia, and other publishers followed or are following suit. Like *Fashion Theory*, *Textile: The Journal of Cloth and Culture* was launched by Berg Publishers in the United Kingdom in 2003. *Critical Studies in Fashion and Beauty* was published by a British publisher, Intellect, in October, 2010. Recently, *The International Journal of Fashion Design, Technology and Education* was launched in 2008, followed by another journal, *Fashion Practice: The Journal of Design, Creative Process and the Fashion Industry*, in 2009; these two journals, which are less theoretical in nature, attempt to cover the full range of contemporary design and manufacture within the context of the fashion industry, and the goal is to bridge the gap between the industry and academia, and the practitioners and the scholars.

Furthermore, the Centre for Fashion Studies was established at Stockholm University in 2006 through a donation from the Erling Persson Family[5] Foundation. The program offers a BA, MA, and a PhD in fashion studies. The Graduate Center of the City University of New York (CUNY) also has an interdisciplinary concentration in fashion studies in conjunction with a PhD program. In September 2010, three schools started a fashion studies program: Parsons The New School for Design in New York is introducing a two-year master's program in fashion studies, Columbia College Chicago in Illinois is starting the new fashion studies department under the

School of Fine and Performing Arts, and the Fashion Institute of Technology is introducing fashion studies as a minor.

Fashion/dress scholars have much to learn from cultural studies, feminist studies, and media studies, all of which may be described as an interdisciplinary area of study, incorporating concepts and methods from cultural anthropology, literature, semiotics, social history, and sociology, among others, as they are interested in how cultural artifacts, including dress and clothing, are produced and reproduced.

OUTLINE OF THE BOOK

This book is intended as an introduction to qualitative research methods in fashion/dress studies for students in any discipline but especially those in the social science discipline who are conducting academic research on fashion/dress using qualitative methods. In addition, those who study fashion design and the business side of fashion, such as merchandising and marketing, could also benefit from this book as it describes the significance of conducting research and also understanding the research processes. Once you know how research in fashion/dress is conducted, you will be able to understand and evaluate the validity and reliability of the studies you read in newspapers, magazines, and/or academic journals, since it is believed that fashion can be studied and analyzed by any layperson because the topic is shallow and nonacademic. The ability to asses a piece as a well-written, research-based article with much depth and substance is intellectually meaningful.

This introductory chapter gives a brief account of fashion studies from a historical perspective and also reviews different concerns about the definitions of the terms "fashion," "dress," or "non-Western dress." It is not easy to grasp the concept of fashion/dress since it is becoming diverse. I trace the development of fashion/dress studies and explain when and who began to take up fashion as their major research area. I explain why fashion should be a concern for academic scholars. The significance of the use of terminologies in a culturally neutral way is discussed along with the idea of making fashion/dress studies an established interdisciplinary field of study that is similar to cultural studies, media studies, or feminist studies.

Chapter 1 explains the link between theory and practice and emphasizes the role that theory plays in every step of the research process. Chapter 2 undertakes a representation of the whole research process and discusses social scientific investigation from initial stages of topic selection and problem formulation through the last phases of analysis. It addresses ways to collect data, methods for assuring the quality of data, the roles researchers enact in the course of their efforts, and how to maintain objectivity before reaching any conclusions. Qualitative designs are by no means uniform, and qualitative researchers pose many diverse questions about the problems they wish to study.

Chapters 3–6 provide major qualitative methods in social sciences and humanities, such as ethnography, survey, semiology, and object-based research, that can be used in the investigation of fashion/dress. Based on various fashion/dress studies literature and empirical case studies included in each methodological explication outlining the major issues and methodological strategies, it becomes evident that fashion can be treated as a material object, an abstract idea, a phenomenon, a system, a cultural value/norm, or an attitude, among many others. In the concluding chapter, future opportunities and directions for fashion/dress studies are explored.

The book includes pedagogical material, such as bullet-point chapter summaries in the beginning of each chapter and suggestions for further reading at the end of the chapter.

CONCLUSION

The writers' personal interests in fashion and dress have evolved into social scientific, empirical research with solid methodological strategies. Fashion/dress scholars continue to make an effort to make it a legitimate field of study in academia by publishing books and academic journals, and at the same time colleges and universities around the world are building fashion studies programs in undergraduate and graduate divisions. This book attempts to raise the awareness of fashion/dress studies by introducing different research methodologies that are also tied to various theoretical approaches.

GUIDE TO FURTHER READING

Baizerman, Suzanne, Joanne B. Eicher, and Catherine Cerny (2008), "Eurocentrism in the Study of Ethnic Dress," in Joanne B. Eicher, Sandra Lee Evenson, and Hazel A. Lutz (eds.), *The Visible Self: Global Perspectives on Dress, Culture, and Society*, pp. 123–32, New York: Fairchild Publications.

Black, Sandy, and Marilyn de Long (eds.) (2009–), *Fashion and Practice: The Journal of Design, Creative Process and the Fashion Industry*, Oxford, UK: Berg.

Carter, Michael (2003), *Fashion Classics from Carlyle to Barthes*, Oxford, UK: Berg.

Eicher, Joanne B., Sandra Lee Evenson, and Hazel A. Lutz (eds.) (2008), *The Visible Self: Global Perspectives on Dress, Culture, and Society*, New York: Fairchild Publications.

Johnson, Kim K. P., Susan J. Torntore, and Joanne B. Eicher (2003), *Fashion Foundations: Early Writings on Fashion and Dress*, Oxford, UK: Berg.

Kaiser, Susan B. (1998), *The Social Psychology of Clothing: Symbolic Appearances in Context*, New York: Fairchild Publications.

Kawamura, Yuniya (2005), *Fashion-ology: An Introduction to Fashion Studies*, Oxford, UK: Berg.

Shin, Kristine (ed.) (2008–), *The International Journal of Fashion Design, Technology and Education*, London: Francis and Taylor.

Steele, Valerie (ed.) (1997–), *Fashion Theory: The Journal of Dress, Body and Culture*, Oxford, UK: Berg.

Tseëlon, Efrat, Ana Marta González, and Susan Kaiser (eds.) (2010–), *Critical Studies in Fashion and Beauty*, Bristol, UK: Intellect.

1 THEORY AND PRACTICE

Objectives

- ■ To understand what a theory is.
- ■ To recognize the purpose of conducting social scientific research.
- ■ To identify the differences between qualitative and quantitative methods.
- ■ To learn how quantitative and qualitative methods are used.
- ■ To distinguish deductive versus inductive research and objective versus subjective approaches.
- ■ To understand how theory and practice are interdependent with each other.
- ■ To learn to apply a symbolic interactionist approach to fashion/dress studies.

Before investigating and understanding different research methods in fashion/dress studies, it is essential that we understand what a theory means and the link between theory and practice. When we say "practice," we mean the practice of research that involves methodological inquiry. This chapter explores the connection between theory and practice/method, which are inextricably linked. Theoretical frameworks, intentions, or purposes with which researchers approach their research not only determine which questions are important but also determine the methods used for social scientific investigation of fashion.

There are different and competing methodologies that are linked to specific theoretical approaches, and they exist side by side in academic discourse. We need to be explicit about the theoretical agendas to which particular methods and practices are attached. I examine predominant theoretical perspectives in social scientific research and discuss how they shape the research done under their theoretical paradigm.

Ideas and thoughts we have can be considered simply guesswork and not scientific knowledge unless they are backed up by research-based facts and evidence (Babbie 1998). The need for facts is one important reason social scientists conduct research. However, the purpose of social research is to check the validity of existing theories about people and society and also to produce information that describes our lives and to develop new theories that explain how our lives are influenced by various social and external forces.

WHAT IS SOCIAL SCIENTIFIC RESEARCH?

Students who research fashion/dress for the first time may think that it has nothing to do with social sciences. However, fashion/dress needs to be studied social scientifically, that is, empirically, in order to earn enough respect in academia because we come across abundant nonacademic information about fashion in our everyday life. They are in magazines, newspapers, catalogues, TV programs, and Internet sites, among many other media sources. Some are subjective opinions and essays on fashion without any reliable sources.

Much of human beings' behaviors, such as the way we dress or the clothing choices we make, are based on assumptions and untested hypotheses. Such untested hypotheses are usually accepted on faith or some common belief and no attempt is made to verify them. In research, we need the objective verification of hypotheses. As Taylor (2005: 3) explains: "The scientific method is designed to discover valid methods of research finding reasons and explanations for controlling natural phenomena which can be replicated." This is what we need to apply to fashion/dress studies.

The fact that we cannot study humans in exactly the same way that we study natural sciences, such as chemistry or physics, can be both a merit and a detriment. One advantage to the social scientists is the ability to pose questions directly to the object of their studies, that is, other humans, and at the same time, this interaction often produces a conscious or unconscious deviation from usual behavior (Babbie 1998). For example, as subjects provide answers to questionnaires or interviews, they know they are being studied and will sometimes try to assist the research effort by supplying answers they believe the researcher is looking for. The subject may treat responses to a questionnaire in a very superficial way. According to Giddens:

> Science is the use of systematic methods of investigation, theoretical thinking, and the logical assessment of arguments to develop a body of knowledge about a particular subject matter. Scientific work depends upon a mixture of boldly innovative thought and the careful marshaling of evidence to support or disconfirm ideas and theories. Information and insights accumulated through scientific study and debate are always to some degree *tentative*—open to being revised, or even completely discarded, in the light of new evidence or arguments. (Giddens 1991: 20)

Science is a logical system that bases knowledge on direct, systematic observation, and its knowledge is based on empirical evidence that is information we can verify with our senses. Empiricism, further discussed in Chapter 2, "Research Process," being concerned with that which can be observed, has always been an ingredient of social sciences. Reliable knowledge comes from that which can be observed and experimented with. The opposite is knowledge based on philosophic speculations that have no scientific grounding, and some believe that fashion/dress studies tend to be in that category.

CONCEPTS/VARIABLES

Social research makes assumptions about the nature of the world as well as people's actions, both of which are predictable, and there are causal relationships. Every event has a constant antecedent, such as why we wear a tank top or a wool sweater. There are external reasons for why we choose to dress in a certain way.

A basic element of science is the *concept,* a mental construct that represents some part of the world in a simplified form. Social scientists use concepts to label various aspects of social life, including "fashion" or "pink" and to classify human begins into different categories, such as gender, social class, or race/ethnicity, and social scientists use them in their theories. A concept can be described as a word or symbol that represents a phenomenon that is a label we use to name and classify our perceptions and experiences, or it can be an abstract idea generalized from particular instances (Collins 1988).

In research, a concept becomes a variable whose value changes from case to case, and it becomes measurable. The use of variables depends on *measurement,* which is a procedure for determining the value of a variable in a specific case. Some variables are easy to measure, such as counting the number of outfits in your wardrobe. However, measuring abstract concepts, such as the level of awareness in the latest fashion trends, as variables can be more difficult.

Researchers, quantitative ones in particular, seek to find how two or more variables are related, and find their correlation, which is the relationship between cause and effect. Correlation means a relationship in which two or more variables change together. Social scientists seek to investigate not just how variables change but why they change (Lather 1986; Maner 1999). Scientists refer to the causal factor as the independent variable and call the effect the dependent variable.

Cause (independent variable) → Effect (dependent variable)

Understanding cause and effect is essential because it allows researchers to predict how one pattern of behavior produces and reproduces another. These linkages explain time order, causality, correlation, description, or explanation, and they can represent any action occurring between the concepts. The connections are generalizations, which are called *theories.*

WHAT IS A THEORY?

The word "theory" is a grand term that is intimidating and frightening to many students and even scholars. It is difficult to grasp and is difficult to comprehend in its entirety in concrete terms since they are not concrete. Theories are found in the social science disciplines of psychology, sociology, anthropology, education, and economics, as well as within many subfields. To locate and read about these theories requires searching literature databases or reviewing guides to the literature about the research topics.

A theory is a generalization about a phenomenon, an explanation of how and why something happens. Therefore, theoretical perspectives are interrelated sets of assumptions, concepts, and propositions that constitute a view of the world (Collins 1988). Theories can be broken into two parts: the things to be connected and the connection itself. They may be concrete and tangible objects, such as a hat, a pair of jeans or shoes, or they can be abstract ideas, such as style, beauty, ugliness, or industries. Frequently, these concepts become linked to even more general theories. Such simple behavior as shopping at a particular store or wearing certain brands can be placed in a larger theoretical framework. Any human social action can be analyzed theoretically.

A theory does not seem to be connected to the real world and our everyday life because of its abstractions. But in fact, our whole way of looking at the world and society depends on our theoretical perspective. Theory and real life, such as a fashion phenomenon and practice, are very much tied together. To read and understand theory is to understand a great deal more about what/who we are and what our world is like. Practical issues actually embody certain theoretical assumptions, and by becoming more aware of them, we become more observant, analytical, and critical.

Theories are embedded in human thought and vary in size, density, abstractedness, completeness, and quality. Many theories are complex and difficult to understand. All scientific theories are speculative to some extent because they are held tentatively as generalizations.[1] But some theories do contribute to the practice they are supposed to inform. Theories can be defined as statements about how things are connected, and their purpose is to explain to and inform us how things are connected, why things happen as they do, including why people dress the way they do. The purpose of a theory is to explain why things happen as they do (Neuman 2000).

Theories help us organize our otherwise disorganized world, make sense of it, guide us how we behave in it or we should behave in it, and also helps us predict what might happen in the future. They are created by developing a set of propositions or generalizations that establish relationships between things in some systematic way and are derived from information that people collect by seeing, hearing, touching, sensing, smelling, and feeling, which is the process of data collection.

According to Creswell (2003), theories develop when researchers test a prediction many times. Researchers combine independent, mediating, and dependent variables based on different forms of measure into hypotheses or research questions. These hypotheses or questions provide information about the type of relationship. When researchers test hypotheses over and over in different settings with different populations, a theory emerges and someone gives it a name. Thus, theory develops as explanation to advance knowledge in particular fields.

DEDUCTION VERSUS INDUCTION/SUBJECTIVITY VERSUS OBJECTIVITY

The deductive-inductive dimension refers to the place of theory in a research study (Flick 1998; Lather 1986). Deductive research begins when a theoretical system develops operational definitions of the propositions and concepts of the theory and matches them empirically to some data. Deductive researchers hope to find data to match a theory while inductive researchers hope to find a theory that explains their data. Inductive research begins with collection of data, such as empirical observations or measurements of some kind, and builds theoretical categories and propositions from relationships discovered among the data. That is, inductive research starts with examination of a phenomenon and then from successive examinations of similar and dissimilar phenomena develops a theory to explain what was studied.

Research designs may also be characterized along a subjective and objective continuum. Ethnography, discussed in Chapter 3, "Ethnography," builds the subjective experiences of both participants and researcher into the research frame, thus providing a depth of understanding often lacking in other approaches to research. In contrast, objective approaches use conceptual categories and explanatory relationships created by the researcher to structure the analysis of particular populations.

THE USE AND PLACEMENT OF THEORY IN QUALITATIVE RESEARCH

According to Creswell (2003), in quantitative research, the hypotheses and research questions are often based on theories that the researcher seeks to test. In qualitative research, the use of theory is more variable. Theory provides an explanation for the variables in questions and hypotheses in quantitative research. In a quantitative dissertation, an entire section of a research proposal might be devoted to explicating the theory for the study. Alternatively, in a qualitative study, the inquirer may generate a theory during a study and place it at the end of a project. But it can come at the beginning and provide a lens that shapes what is looked at and the questions asked (Flick 1998). In mixed methods research, researchers may both test theories and generate them (Neuman 2000). Moreover, mixed methods research may contain a theoretical lens, such as a focus on feminist, racial, or class issues, that guides the entire study.

In qualitative theory, theory becomes the end point for a study. It is an inductive process of building from the data to broad themes to a generalized model or theory. The researcher begins by gathering detailed information from participants and forms this information into categories or themes. These themes or categories are developed into broad patterns, theories, or generalizations that are then compared with personal experiences or with existing literature on the topic (Flick 1998).

Some place theory at the center of the qualitative research process and suggest a process that revolves around and draws from theory during the various stages of research. In ethnography, for instance, fieldworkers do not necessarily need the prior specification of a theory because it may introduce premature closure on the issues to be investigated and also lead researchers away from the views of participants in a social setting. Such qualitative researchers may prefer not to be committed in advance to developing the theoretical implications of their work in any particular direction, and they believe that this should flow from the emerging data.

Qualitative researchers should at least briefly explain the approach they used, and the ways in which they interpreted their early data, and how preliminary findings influenced subsequent data gathering and analysis. Some of them at times follow an analytic induction model, and they are guided by general hypotheses before collecting their data. These hypotheses are then revised as the data emerge and as the analysis proceeds. They can challenge or enlarge an existing theory or strike out in a new direction with a new theory.

UNDERSTANDING THE MEANING
OF A FASHION THEORY

There is no one fashion theory per se that is universally accepted, and since fashion/dress studies requires various perspectives, approaches, and interpretations, there are multiple fashion theories that rely on major social theories. Fashion theory draws a wide range of theoretical orientations such as structural functionalism, conflict theory, or symbolic interactionism, among many others, just like feminist theory or cultural studies theory.

According to Lillethun (2007: 77), academic disciplines engaged in theorizing fashion include, but are not limited to, humanities (art and design history), social sciences (anthropology, area and ethnic studies, cultural studies, economics, geography, history, psychology, and sociology), business (marketing, merchandising, and retailing), and fashion programs, which are interdisciplinary by nature. Pedersen, Buckland, and

Bates (2008–2009) discuss and define the concept of "theory," making an attempt to integrate developed theories into fashion/dress studies and explore the intricate relationship between theory and dress scholarship. Barnard also points out:

> Fashion/dress scholars come up with different theories of fashion based on their academic training. Each discipline has its own set or sets of ideas and conceptual frameworks in terms of which it defines, analyses and explains fashion. Each discipline, then, comes with its own theory, or theories, in terms of which it goes about the task of studying fashion. (Barnard 2007a: 7)

Fashion theory should be no different from any other theory in any field of academic research. It attempts to generalize human behavior that is related to fashion/dress. The awareness of the importance in establishing a theoretical framework in addition to the deep understanding of methodological strategies must be emphasized in fashion/dress studies, as Lipovetsky insists that fashion has "provoked no serious theoretical dissension" (1994: 4). Tseëlon (2001: 436) explains: "Research in fashion appears to be, for the most part, data-driven and theory-free. Having failed to form an integrated body of knowledge, it rarely uses theory as a springboard to formulate research questions. Rather, theory seems to be an add-on, not an integral part of the research question generation." Tseëlon also finds problems in methods:

> Method use in fashion studies is contradictory and comprises a mixture of unempirical and overtly technical applications. On the one hand, most work on fashion as a social and cultural phenomenon is theoretical. It abounds with folkwisdom but lacks an empirical backing for its theoretical and common-sense views. It relies, instead, on anecdotal evidence for illustration purposes. On the other hand, method is not seen as a means of generating insight. (Tseëlon 2001: 436)

Coming up with an intriguing and worthwhile research question or hypothesis is one thing, and deciding the most appropriate research method/s is another. As explained earlier, the method adopted in your research is linked to a certain theoretical underpinning.

Lillethun explains:

> [A] theory consists of a conceptual network of propositions that explain an observable phenomenon. While fashion is an "observable phenomenon," at this time no comprehensive theory of fashion has been universally accepted. Instead, concepts and propositions concerning fashion have been suggested from a variety of disciplinary perspectives.…We understand fashion theory as inquiry into fundamental questions about fashion with the objectives of understanding, explaining and predicting fashion change. (Lillethun 2007: 77)

TWO MAJOR THEORETICAL PERSPECTIVES: MACRO AND MICRO

Before confusing your mind with multiple, abstract theories, the most fundamental way to look at different theoretical perspectives is at the macro and the micro levels (Collins 1988; Giddens 1991). Students who take Introductory Sociology are introduced to major social theories in the beginning of the semester. It is important that students in fashion/dress studies also learn major theoretical perspectives before they embark on their own research in fashion/dress studies. Broadly speaking, social theories have two camps: macro, which is a deductive approach, and micro, which is an inductive approach.

As indicated earlier, theory influences our choice of research method. Functionalists and conflict theorists with a macro perspective tend to use quantitative methods while symbolic interactionists with a micro perspective tend to use qualitative methods. In deductive, quantitative research, theory plays a big role at the beginning of research and the theory may be revised at the end based on the findings while in inductive, qualitative research, it plays a role after the data is collected and the research makes an attempt to make sense of the data collected.

Theoretical Perspective	Methods	Approach
Macro-structuralism	Quantitative	Deductive
Micro-interactionism	Qualitative	Inductive

Theoretical perspectives are divided clearly between those perspectives that are concerned with the large-scale characteristics of social structure known as macro structuralism and those concerned with person-to-person encounters and the details of human interaction and communication known as micro interactionism.

There is also the combination of micro and macro known as meso that incorporates both levels of analysis as well as methodological strategies, which is explained in Chapter 7, "Other Methodologies." Neuman (2000) reviews theories at three levels: micro-level, meso-level, and macro-level. Micro-level theories provide explanations limited to small slices of time, space, or numbers of people, such as the types of gifts teenagers buy for their parents during Christmas or designers' interaction with publicists during the fashion week. Meso-level theories link the micro and macro levels. There are theories of organizations, social movements, or communities; for example, a broad social network among well-known designers can be studied from a meso perspective by analyzing how the network is structured, which is a macro perspective, and how each individual designer is connected with others personally or professionally, which is a micro perspective.

Macro-level theories explain larger aggregates, for instance, American consumers' shopping/spending behavior during recession, or the impact of what a celebrity wears in the media in retail sales.

In quantitative studies, one uses theory deductively and places it toward the beginning of the plan for a study. With the objective of testing or verifying a theory rather than developing it, the researcher advances a theory, collects data to test it, and reflects on the confirmation and disconfirmation of the theory by the results. The theory becomes a framework for the entire study, an organizing model for the research questions or hypotheses and for the data collection procedure.

The three theoretical lenses can be combined to incorporate mixed methods. Mixed methods studies may include theory deductively in theory testing and verification, or inductively as in an emerging theory or pattern. In either situation, the use of theory may be directed by the emphasis on either quantitative or qualitative approaches in the mixed methods research (Creswell 2003). Therefore researchers who use the combined methods use theory either deductively (as in quantitative research) or inductively (as in qualitative research).

THEORY AND METHODS

There are various theories as well as various research methods that can be used. Different theories demand different research methods and vice versa. A research method is a systematic plan for doing research. In this book, I am discussing ethnography, survey methods, semiology, and object-based research. The first two are obtrusive and the last two are unobtrusive measures. There is the link between methodological orientations and theory. In general, each of the two ways is related to one of the theoretical approaches. The scientific orientation corresponds to the structural-functional approach, the interpretive orientation to the symbolic interaction approach. For a macro-structural perspective, the researcher gathers empirical, ideally quantitative data while for a micro-interactionist perspective, the researcher develops a qualitative account of the subjective sense people make of their world.

Empirical findings are always theory-laden if they are necessarily produced by or only make sense in the context of a particular theory; they are usually not theory-neutral. Theories can stand by themselves although they are broadly general and abstract. Practice or empiricism, if left alone by itself, will simply be a story, and this is what happens with fashion/dress–related information. Therefore, it needs to be described analytically and put into theoretical perspective. Thus these two are indispensable to each other and are tightly linked to each other and cannot be separated in conducting a research study. Some start with setting out a theoretical framework while others do it the other way around. Building empirically grounded theory requires a reciprocal relationship between data and theory (Lather 1986: 267). Data-collecting sources in qualitative research such as interviews and observations cannot be validated as easily as traditional quantitative data sources that yield numerical measurements, but the reliability in the qualitative research can be controlled by keeping careful records of interviews and observations.

QUALITATIVE AND QUANTITATIVE METHODS

The field of social sciences is split between advocates of quantitative methods and those who favor qualitative or purely verbal theory. Members of the former camp tend to dismiss the latter as "nonscientific" or merely "philosophical," while those on the other side attack their opponents as "positivists" following an outmoded vision of science and as practitioners of methods without substance since what they have is only the numbers on paper (Collins 1988).

Before about 1965, the scientific side was the mainstream in American sociology, although its methods were not yet much put into practice but were regarded as the path toward progress in the future. Technical sophistication in mathematics and statistics has increased a great deal at a fast pace since then, but the weight of intellectual opinion, especially among theorists, has swung the other way. There used to be considerable hostility between what is seen as the methodological-quantitative side of the field and the theoretical-qualitative side. Many social scientists have been attracted to French structuralism, social phenomenology, ethnomethodology, and other positions that are openly against traditional science. Interpretive approaches, such as historical sociology, which is nonquantitative, became popular.

Since fashion/dress studies as an intellectual field is new compared to other disciplines that had existed for centuries, qualitative and verbal formulations are better suited to getting ahold of the main outlines of what we are dealing with. Instead of setting out a theory and finding data that suits the theory, we can observe fashion/dress as a phenomenon/practice or study clothes as objects and find a theory that emerges out of it. If you are new to fashion/dress studies as a researcher, taking a symbolic interactionist theoretical framework with an interpretive approach is the best start.

FASHION/DRESS STUDIES FROM A SYMBOLIC INTERACTIONIST PERSPECTIVE

This is one of several theoretical schools of thought in the social sciences, and it involves a set of related propositions that describes and explains certain aspects of human behavior. What humans say and do are the results of how they interpret their social world. Human behavior depends on learning rather than biological instinct. The theory, therefore, emphasizes the importance of social and external forces imposed on human behavior. Human beings communicate what they learn through symbols, the most common system of symbols being language, which is verbal symbols. The job of a symbolic interactionist is to capture the essence of this process of interpreting or attaching meaning to various symbols, verbal or nonverbal. Fashion/dress studies scholars are primarily interested in the nonverbal dimension of this theory since clothing is a nonverbal mode of communication.

The basis of symbolic interactionism is rooted in John Dewey's (1859–1952) work on social behavior, along with Charles Horton Cooley (1864–1929), W. I. Thomas (1863–1947), and Robert Ezra Park (1864–1944).[2] It was George Herbert Mead (1863–1931) in particular who studied social interaction as a dynamic process. Mead's student Herbert Blumer (1900–1987) is considered the founder of symbolic interactionism, and he coined the term, referring to many of Mead's concepts and theories that consist of the idea of interaction as a process of people sharing meanings and fitting their lines of action together. According to Blumer (1969b), meanings derive from the social process of people or groups of people interacting. People create their realities through different interpretations and meanings. Blumer applied this to fashion processes as well (1969a). Erving Goffman, a student of Blumer's at the University of Chicago, was influenced by symbolic interactionism and wrote *The Presentation of Self in Everyday Life* (1959), which examines the social significance of one's physical appearance, and his study is often applied in fashion/dress studies. Similarly, Gregory Stone (1962) applies the symbolic interactionist perspective to analyze appearance, which is important in developing and maintaining the self. Fred Davis (1992) is another scholar who discusses the symbolic significance of fashion in communication and interactive process and explains the ambivalent nature of fashion.

Social roles, institutional structures, rules, norms, goals, and the like may provide the materials with which individuals create their definitions, but these elements do not by themselves determine what the definitions will be or how individuals will act. In essence, symbolic interactionism emphasizes social interactions (action with symbolic meaning), negotiation of definitions, and emphatic role-taking between humans. Symbolic interactionists work within the interpretive sociological tradition following Max Weber's interpretive sociology that emphasizes the importance of subjective meaning in the social organization of everyday life.

MAX WEBER'S THEORY OF *VERSTEHEN* (INTERPRETATIVE) SOCIOLOGY

Humans do not simply move about. We engage in meaningful action. A second type of research is interpretive sociology, the study of society that focuses on the meanings people attach to their social world. Max Weber, the pioneer of this framework, argues that the proper focus of sociology is interpretation, that is, *verstehen,* or understanding the meaning people create in their everyday lives. *Verstehen* means understanding in German. It is the interpretive sociologist's job not just to observe what people do but also to share in their world of meaning, coming to appreciate why they act as they do. Subjective thoughts and feelings, all of which science tends to dismiss as a personal bias, should/can move to the center of the researcher's attention.

Weber argued that human social life is, in some ways, different from other features of the natural world. Human beings are frequently rational and organize their efforts to reach intended goals. The observer must consider the behavior from the viewpoint of the actor.

Weber writes:

> Sociology...is a science concerning itself with the interpretive understanding of social action and thereby with a causal explanation of its course and consequences. We shall speak of "action" insofar as the acting individual attaches a subjective meaning to his behavior—be it overt or covert, omission or acquiescence. Action is "social" insofar as its subjective meaning takes account of the behavior of others and is thereby oriented in its course. (Weber 1978 [1909]: 4)

Weber says "all explanations must establish adequacy on the level of meaning" (Weber 1968: 12), and Muggleton is one of the fashion scholars who applies Weberian interpretation of meaning to his study of a subcultural phenomena while stressing the significance of subjectivity and also the social factors that influence the meanings that each individual creates. Muggleton writes:

> [A] Weberian study of subcultures must be based upon an interpretation of the subjectively held meanings, values and beliefs of the subculturalists themselves. This is the premise upon which Weber's *verstehen* methodology is founded, the literal translation of the term *verstehen* being "human understanding"....We must therefore take seriously the subjective meanings of subculturalists, for these provide the motivation for their conduct. This makes the subjective dimension a central component in any explanation of social phenomena. (Muggleton 2000: 10)

He continues:

> A Weberian explanation of subcultures must therefore be adequate on the levels of both meaning and causality: it should begin with an empirical investigation of the subjective values of individual subculturalists, but go beyond the level of actors' meanings "to the collective forces that impel the actor" (Ritzer 1981: 80), to identify the belief systems that have played a part in the emergence of subcultural phenomena. (Muggleton 2000: 10)

While Muggleton is in support of Weber's *verstehen* methodology, he is also looking at a subcultural phenomenon from a macro-structural point of view. Social structure is never empty, and there are always individuals that belong within the structure. There is an underlying implication of the meso analysis in his study, which is the interaction between the macro and the micro levels.

CONCLUSION

Fashion/dress studies needs to be studied theoretically and empirically. Theoretical perspectives vary depending on the researcher's choice of methods, disciplinary affiliation, and background training. Different research questions demand different theories and different methodological inquiries, quantitative or qualitative. The fundamental perspective to understanding a theory is the micro-, meso-, and macro-levels of analysis, and qualitative methods often take a micro-interactionist approach that can be applied to fashion/dress studies. Theory appears as an end point of a qualitative study, a pattern or a generalization that emerges inductively from data collection and analysis.

GUIDE TO FURTHER READING

Berger, Arthur Asa (1992), *Reading Matter: Multidisciplinary Perspectives on Material Culture,* New Brunswick, NJ: Transaction Publishers.

Blumer, Herbert (1969a), "Fashion: From Class Differentiation to Collective Selection," *The Sociological Quarterly,* 10/3: 275–91.

Blumer, Herbert (1969b), *Symbolic Interactionism: Perspective and Method,* Englewood Cliffs, NJ: Prentice-Hall.

Buzzi, Stella, and Gibson, Pamela Church (eds.) (2001), *Fashion Cultures: Theories, Explorations, Analysis,* London: Routledge.

Collins, Randall (1988), *Theoretical Sociology,* San Diego, CA: Harcourt Brace Javanovich.

Lillethun, Abby (2007), "Introduction," in Linda Welters and Abby Lillethun (eds.), *The Fashion Reader,* pp. 77–82, Oxford, UK: Berg.

Neuman, W. Lawrence (2000), *Social Research Methods: Qualitative and Quantitative Approaches* (4th edn), Boston: Allyn and Bacon.

Pedersen, Elaine L., Sandra S. Buckland, and Christina Bates (2008–2009), "Theory and Dress Scholarship: A Discussion on Developing and Applying Theory," *Dress: The Annual Journal of the Costume Society of America,* 35: 71–85.

2 RESEARCH PROCESS

Objectives

- To understand the entire research process in fashion/dress studies.
- To learn the meaning of objectivity and empiricism in social sciences.
- To recognize where and when subjectivity comes in.
- To explain every step of the research process from the topic selection, problem formulation, data collection to data analysis, and conclusion.
- To learn how to evaluate Internet sources and to avoid plagiarism.
- To recognize ethical issues and the Institutional Review Board (IRB).

The term "research" is often used very loosely in everyday life just like the term "fashion" or "dress." But in conducting research on fashion/dress, we must understand what processes it has to go through and what conditions are required. What exactly is research? How are we supposed to research fashion/dress? In order for us to conduct solid, in-depth research, it is essential that we know the entire research process in detail and step by step and go over each step carefully.

In this chapter, a representation of the whole research process is examined, and social scientific investigation from the initial stage of topic selection and research question formulation through the last phases of analysis, such as analytical interpretation and drawing conclusions, is discussed in detail. Some practical suggestions for conducting research are also explained. Who, what, where, when, why, and how are the basic questions that need to be posed. What kinds of data are needed and from whom can we get them? Where can the data be found? When is it accessible or conveniently obtained? How should it be recorded, collected, or stored? Why is it needed anyway? What does it add to a study and do we have the resources to collect it? Some of the ethical issues that may appear in research, the establishment of the Institutional Review Board (IRB), and concerns for plagiarism are also explored in this chapter.

Some of the answers to research questions are often taken for granted, but as Lazarsfeld and Rosenberg (1957) explain, after the fact, common sense is capable of explaining or providing a rationale for almost anything, but before the facts are known, common sense supports all manner of contradictory conjecture. Common sense can often be vague and even wrong.

Specific qualitative research methods are discussed more in detail in subsequent chapters. Most qualitative data are text, and thus narrative data from interviews, questionnaires, protocols, field notes, diaries, minutes of meetings, and other records should be maintained as accurately as possible. I also examine to what extent an individual researcher affects research design, findings, and interpretations. The role and experience of the researcher must be taken into consideration. The premise is that if procedures are applied precisely and documented exactly, then anyone with similar training can replicate a study, and therefore, social science can be conducted with no concern for individual variation in researchers. It emphasizes the goal of objectivity in social sciences.

OBJECTIVITY AND EMPIRICISM

Before beginning research and collecting data, it is extremely important to keep in mind the two most important features of social scientific research. Whatever the research topic may be, whether it is fashion/dress or something else, if you are conducting serious research, objectivity and empiricism need to be taken into consideration (Giddens 1991). While it is occasionally difficult to maintain them faithfully, the researcher's awareness is crucial in attempting to come up with unbiased results at the end.

OBJECTIVITY/VALUE-NEUTRALITY

Both quantitative and qualitative researchers know that social science research should maintain an unbiased neutral position. Social scientists are expected to study the world around them as external researchers while putting their own personal values aside.

Objectivity means the ability of a researcher to articulate what the procedures are so that others can repeat the research if they so choose. You do your research, explain your methods and articulate the results, and basically inform others that they can repeat the study. If the researcher's findings and analysis were correct, subsequent research will corroborate this. And if they were false or inaccurate, that will be shown in subsequent research. However, we all know that no research is completely absolute or accurate without any flaws, and there is always some room for doubts or skepticism that can be challenged, but every researcher is making a contribution to the research community within his or her particular field, such as fashion/dress studies.

Therefore, a guiding principle of scientific study is objectivity or personal neutrality in conducting research. The idea of objective research is to allow the facts to speak for themselves and not become colored by the personal values and biases of the researcher. In reality, of course, achieving total neutrality is impossible for anyone. But carefully observing the rules of scientific research can maximize objectivity.

Max Weber (1864–1920), a German scholar, notes that people choose value-relevant research topics that they care about personally, but he cautioned that once their work is underway, researchers should try their best to be value-free. We must be dedicated to finding truth as it is rather than as we think it should be. Researchers should stay open-minded and be willing to accept whatever results come from their work, whether they like them or not. Weber's argument still carries much weight in social sciences, although most researchers admit that we can never be completely value-free or get rid of all our biases. Whether we are professionally trained in research or not, we are influenced by our social backgrounds and personal experiences, and this is something that is difficult to deny (Weber 1949).

Therefore, although the goal of social scientific investigation is often said to be objective knowledge, emotional detachment, free of bias or prejudice, we question to what extent this is possible since the researchers are human beings with feelings. Can human beings become completely objective once they are trained in social sciences? While some scholars believe that objectivity in social sciences is absolutely necessary and possible, there are those who argue that it is not possible, especially in qualitative methods. Some argue that one may have to compromise objectivity in qualitative research.

From a phenomenological perspective,[1] any judgments are subjective, being influenced by the actor's own experiences. All empirical observations are necessarily theory-laden, and the choice of a theory is a subjective one. All members of society have different values, any researcher unconsciously but necessarily has his or her own argument affected by his or her personal values. But this does not mean that quantitative methods that deal with statistical data can maintain absolute objectivity since that is also based on the subjective decision in terms of the variables and the raw data selected.

EMPIRICISM

Empiricism is the second important feature in social scientific research, and it asserts that knowledge comes from experience in the formation of ideas while rejecting the notion of innate ideas. Only the information gathered applying your senses is used to make decisions. Empiricism became popular in the eighteenth and nineteenth centuries with the emergence of science, and researchers who denounce qualitative methods often equate empiricism with science. This is known as an epistemological view,[2] based on the assumption that the only source of knowledge is experience. In social sciences, it is used positively to describe that style of research that tries to avoid untested theoretical speculation and to aim always at the provision of quantitative, empirical evidence. Some of the criticisms are that empiricism tends to reduce the importance of theory on the one hand and on the other, underestimates the technical and theoretical difficulties of gathering reliable data.

However, qualitative experience can also be called empirical since empiricism is something we experience and feel using our physical senses, such as hearing, watching, observing, touching, smelling, and maybe even tasting (Flick 1998). For any empirical research, there are methodological strategies. As explained in Chapter 1, "Theory and Practice," theory and practice are therefore discussed side by side as they complement each other, and there is an inseparable link between the two. Theories explain a set of empirical observations, and they function as analytical tools; they are abstract and make generalizations while searching for patterns in human behavior. Practice or empiricism is atheoretical and is more specific with concrete research methods involved.

RESEARCH PROCESS

A researcher cannot suddenly jump into the data collection process. There is a planning stage; the whole process of research needs to be considered and reconsidered before you begin your research and organize and structure your study (Marshall and Rossman 1999; Maner 1999; Neuman 2000).

SELECTING A TOPIC

The very first step of research is a topic selection. You know you want to research and write about fashion/dress, but that is an extremely broad topic. Your research focus needs to be more specific than simply "fashion/dress." You know that you want to research something related to or relevant to fashion, but what about fashion? Fashion/dress can be analyzed from numerous perspectives, and you should know exactly what area of fashion you want to study and what exactly you are trying to investigate in your research.

Furthermore, you must be able to clearly state the topic you are interested in and raise the problem you want to investigate. Many students flounder in developing a researchable topic because they fail to develop a clear research problem/question statement. Raising a clear research statement or a problem statement allows you to concentrate on the topic and exclude everything else that is irrelevant.

It is desirable to consider and describe any theories that have implications for understanding the topic. Consider brainstorming a list of possible topics. The purpose of brainstorming is to produce ideas uncritically. After brainstorming, you then need to critically evaluate the ideas generated in order to select an appropriate topic for review. Occasionally, combining various ideas and thoughts during brainstorming can produce a useful topic.

Subjective Interests in Fashion/Dress

While many researchers explain why the topic has any research meaning and significance in the research community, there are usually other personal reasons why they are studying fashion/dress. It may even be simply "because I like shopping for clothes," which few fashion/dress researchers would publically admit. If you are in the position to decide a research topic, the selected topic must have some value and importance to you. Then it is entirely a subjective decision since it is based on your own subjective feelings of importance and possibly on your personal experience. Can a subjective process be objective? Most probably not. Our own cultural background, academic training, life experiences, and individual personal traits could have a profound effect not only on the topic selection but also on the research process and even on the findings. Sex, age, ethnicity, religion, country of origin, economic status, and social or occupational roles can shape the questions researchers ask. An inquiry process is affected not only by personal characteristics but also by a researcher's personal history and family background, and thus the researcher needs to make assumptions accordingly. While consideration of personal interests is important, we need to make sure that the topic selected is well within the boundaries expected by the research community.

Muggleton in his research explains why and how he was involved in the study of subculture by referring to Weber's idea of value-relevance:

> According to Max Weber (1864–1920), all sociology is necessarily "value-relevant" (Weber 1949) in that the selection of a research topic, the decision to investigate particular aspects over others, and the logic and method of enquiry employed are all inevitably grounded in the subjective values of the researcher. A useful way of introducing this book might therefore be to "come clean" about my own personal reasons for writing it. From 1976 onwards, I became increasingly involved in the emerging provincial punk rock scene. I took on certain aspects of the subculture's dress codes, jettisoning my flares for "straights," platforms for trainers, and my bright orange, wing-collared shirt and fat knot tie for a white button-down brinylon museum piece worn with a stripy school tie left hanging at half mast. (Muggleton 2000: 1)

Therefore, Muggleton calls his approach "neo-Weberian" since it is located within the tradition of conventional qualitative sociology that derives from Weber's insistence upon the need of sociological explanations to recognize the subjective goals, values, and motivations of social actors (Muggleton 2000: 5).

Similarly, when I look back and ask how I got involved in this area of research as a fashion scholar, it is very personal. First of all, my grandmother sewed her own kimono, my mother studied at a fashion school and is a very creative person. As I grew up watching my mother making clothes and knitting as a hobby, it was very natural for me to do the same. I have loved designing clothes since I was a child. I love sewing and making clothes. I decided to enroll myself in a fashion school at the age of twenty-one as I was graduating from a university while my classmates were all looking for jobs. I am professionally trained as a fashion designer. A career transition from a fashion designer to a fashion scholar may be quite a change, but I am still involved in fashion nonetheless. Although I was mostly educated in the West (elementary school in Australia and high school in Austria), I am Japanese by heritage, and thus I have always been aware of the famous Japanese designers in Paris, such as Kenzo, Issey Miyake, Rei Kawakubo, and Yohji Yamamoto. As a result, I conducted my research and wrote my doctoral dissertation on the Japanese designers in Paris. There is nothing objective about the selection process of my topic while I was very aware of the importance of objectivity, putting aside my personal interests and values, during my research in Paris.[3]

Therefore, whichever topic is selected, it often comes from the researcher's personal interests and experiences that are far from objectivity. Those of us who are fashion scholars often like fashion in various ways, whether it is because they understand the technical aspects of design, or they simply love buying new clothes every season. However, the researchers must be aware that the subjective interests and biases must stop at the first level of topic selection. From there, you need an objective perspective to analyze and interpret fashion/dress.

You begin with an idea for a research study. You know you want to study something about fashion/dress or something in relation to that. You begin reading the related and relevant literature on the topic/idea. During this process, you should begin to formulate a research question or a hypothesis. It is acceptable if your research question changes during the research process when your methodological tools are qualitative. This is one of the major differences between quantitative and qualitative methods.

Sociological Imagination

Your personal interests in fashion and dress are all part of the larger social picture if you apply "sociological imagination," which is a phrase coined by C. Wright Mills (2000 [1959]). Using the sociological imagination means recognizing the connection between individual, private experience and the wider society. Mills calls the personal level an individual's "biography," and he uses the term "history" to refer to patterns and relationships on the larger scale of society. You have individual feelings and attitudes about fashion, current trends, and the way you or others dress. These make your personal, biographical experience of your life as an individual. Applying sociological imagination to your life expands your perspective, and it allows you to see yourself as well as others in a larger, more complex picture. You can begin to see where your experience as a person who likes fashion fits into the social world in which you live, the history of which your biography is a part. It could be that you are part of the wider fashion system in a particular fashion city or you may represent yourself in a new occupational category of fashion. Therefore, according to Mills (2000 [1959]), to use sociological imagination is to identify the intersection of biography and history, the ways in which people are affected by social forces and social groups are affected by their members.

THE LITERATURE REVIEW

Once you know your research topic, questions, or hypothesis, the next step is the literature review. This step is required for any scholarly research paper and cannot be avoided. There are two purposes to the literature review:

1. You do not want to needlessly duplicate another researcher's ideas or research, although sometimes researchers conduct the same or similar studies to check the reliability of results. A thorough literature review helps you learn from previous research, give recognition where credit is due, become more knowledgeable about the problem or the question you are studying and thus avoid unnecessary duplication of effort.
2. You refer to other studies and research so that you know what has been done in the field, what other research questions were raised and answered. It shows to the readers that you have done your homework before embarking on your own study. It is considered preliminary research. It is not sufficient to simply focus on your own research. Your own research should not even begin without the literature review. It is important to understand that every researcher is making a contribution to the research community or the community of fashion/dress studies.

The literature review is a combination of the literature on a topic you select. In order to create an original work, you need to review various ideas and findings in the literature. You may locate and read literature in academic journals, books, and even on the Internet. It is best to consult a librarian for appropriate databases that you can use for your topic. Your literature review must be listed alphabetically in the bibliography pages at the very end of the book or paper, and many scholars use them as references. They also look to see whether you have covered the basic literature for the topic you have selected. It is used to support the legitimacy of one's research questions, appropriateness of design, the theoretical underpinnings of the study, and the validity of conclusions.

CHOOSING APPROPRIATE RESEARCH METHOD/S

Broadly speaking, there are quantitative and qualitative methods as indicated earlier. The differences and commonalities are discussed in Chapter 1, "Theory and Practice." Many fashion/dress studies use primarily qualitative methods as they often refer to material objects and visual materials as evidence and also observe how people are dressed. From Chapters 3 to 7 in this book, various qualitative research methods, such as ethnography and questionnaires among others, are introduced and explained in depth. We need to remember that no method is perfect or absolute so the researchers need to be aware of the limitations of their studies and their research methodologies and also to assess the weaknesses and strengths of each method. Methods you incorporate do not have to be just one. Multiple methods can be combined to try to answer your research question; different studies integrating two or more methods are discussed in Chapter 6, "Object-based Research" and Chapter 7, "Other Methodologies."

Purpose of Using Qualitative Research Methods

It was not until the beginning of the eighteenth century that research in the social sciences began. The social sciences were modeled after the physical sciences and attempts were made to make the social sciences as objective as the physical sciences. Around the middle of the twentieth century, qualitative research methods were being explored for use in the social sciences.

Many researchers and scholars do not clearly indicate what their methodological strategies are, and thus a reader must assume and read between the lines that certain methods were utilized in executing their research. Interestingly, graduate students' doctoral dissertations and the books based on them often have explanations on methods.

We know that, broadly speaking, there are quantitative and qualitative research methods in the world of academic research. Qualitative and quantitative data inform each other and produce insight and understanding in a way that cannot be duplicated by either approach. Some research problems simply cannot be addressed adequately by any other methods except ethnography or interviews, for example. While many quantitative researchers tend to dismiss qualitative methods, such as observation or participant observation, as a legitimate method, they have begun to reconsider their standpoint.

In this book, the qualitative methods that qualitatively oriented researchers often employ and administer in studying and analyzing fashion-related practices and events are discussed. I do not intend to dismiss quantitative methods entirely. We should be aware of what quantitative methods are and the differences between the two methods used in studying fashion and dress.

Qualitative analysis refers to analysis that is not based on precise measurement and mathematical claims. Fashion/dress–related analysis is frequently qualitative because research goals often involve the understanding of phenomena in ways that do not require quantification, or because the phenomena do not lend themselves to precise measurements. You cannot give any numbers to fashion phenomena. For instance, in participant observation, the researcher may simply aim to observe people's behavior without counting instances of particular behavior while in other cases, such as historical research, the records may be inadequate for precise quantitative measurements even if that was the research goal.

RESEARCH SETTING AND APPROPRIATE RESEARCH POPULATION/SUBJECT

As in any other research situation, you must determine how broad an area of social world is covered. In most research, this decision is largely dictated by the research question and the nature of the research problem under investigation. It has to be clear in the mind of a researcher who is included in the study. During the research design phase of a project, the researcher needs to consider a rationale for identifying and using a particular setting as a site for data collection. A decision must be made regarding who serves as the researcher and the research study population. The research site or setting should be a location where entry is possible and the target population is available. You must carefully identify an appropriate population, not merely an easily accessible one.

The research question is generally regarded as the primary guide to the appropriate research site selection. If the researcher's question has to do with French Haute Couture and couturières, the data collection site has to be some place related to that and you must find individuals related to that. It is less likely that you can conduct such a research in Asia. Typically, the decision to use a particular research site is tied closely to obtaining access to an appropriate population of potential subjects. Poor study site selection and poor sample decisions may weaken or ruin eventual findings.

Sampling Strategies

In the case of administering a questionnaire, which is discussed in Chapter 4, "Survey Methods," rarely do you have the luxury of studying an entire population. It is difficult to know if your classroom of 100 students is representative of other classes on your campus or in your state or elsewhere. Constraints of time and economic cost demand a technique to reduce a population to a manageable size. If you randomly sample 500 students out of a student body of 20,000, it means that each student has an equal chance of being selected as one of the 500. If all of the potential respondents do not have the same probability of being included, the result is a biased sample.

The logic of using a sample of subjects is to make inferences about some larger population from a smaller one, the sample. In quantitative research, the researcher is keenly concerned with probability sampling (Fowler 2002; Thompson 2002). The concept of probability sampling is based on the notion that a sample can be selected that will mathematically represent subgroups of some larger population. In probability sampling strategies, there are simple random sampling, systematic random sampling, and stratified random sampling.[4]

Various types of samplings and many related issues are involved with the statistical analysis of population samples. Different statistical techniques for making comparisons require assumptions that you learn to evaluate when you consider the appropriateness of different statistical techniques available for the problem you are studying (Thompson 2002). Understanding sampling, issues of size, and statistical techniques are important to enable anyone to make informed judgments about the claims other people make about research they have conducted on various issues. Although qualitative researchers are not directly involved in the statistical analysis, they can choose their research sampling in survey methods.

Snowball Sampling

This is a nonprobability sampling strategy known as snowball sampling, and it is occasionally the way to locate subjects with certain attributes or characteristics necessary in a study. Snowball samples are particularly popular among researchers interested in studying various classes of deviance, sensitive topics, or difficult-to-reach populations (Thompson 2002). The basic strategy of snowballing involves first identifying several people with relevant characteristics and interviewing them or having them answer a questionnaire. These subjects are then asked for the names of other people who possess the same attributes as they do. Similar people flock together. If you are a designer, your friends are usually designers. If you work as a buyer, you do have a connection with other buyers. In my study on Japanese designers in Paris (2004), I used the method of snowballing to locate Japanese designers in Paris who were otherwise difficult to locate. I first contacted a couple of Japanese designers in Paris who were taking part in the Paris Fashion Collection and interviewed them. Then I asked each of them to refer me to one or two Japanese designers or individuals who live and work in the fashion industry in Paris. By asking these first subjects for referrals of additional people, I found that the sample eventually "snowballs" from a few subjects to many subjects.

COLLECTING DATA

Once you decide which method/s to employ, you start collecting your data. The word "data" is not necessarily quantitative. Anything and everything that is collected throughout your research, such as the field notes, answers to your questionnaire, and photographs, among others, is considered your data. Whichever method/s you choose, you now actually put that into practice. Make sure you keep good records of your research as you will use them for the next stage in analyzing the results of your collected data. Specific data collection methods in qualitative research are discussed in subsequent chapters of this book.

MAKING AN ANALYSIS OF THE DATA

Any data analysis begins with a review of the research proposal or plans with which the work began. It can take a month or two to organize and sort the data collected. Filing papers, making neat stack of tapes, putting interviews in order, and organizing documents and artifacts are necessary before starting your constructive data analysis. This is a must component of the research project. Many researchers wander and deviate from the original question set in the beginning, so you need to revisit and relocate the question/s. In qualitative research, you do not code or elicit meaning from statistical data.

DRAWING CONCLUSIONS

You discuss what can be concluded from your research on fashion/dress. Were you able to prove or disprove the hypothesis you set up in the beginning of your research? Did you find anything that you did not know before this research? Is there a theoretical or empirical contribution of your research in fashion/dress studies? At this stage, you are probably writing a report, an article, or a book, and as you draw conclusions of your study, you are raising further questions in the future for fashion/dress scholars.

EVALUATING INTERNET SOURCES

Since the 1990s, the advent of the Internet has brought enormous changes in our lives. Today practically no one can avoid the impact of the Internet that has permeated throughout the world. The community of academics and researchers has also changed dramatically, and therefore, the researchers should be able to evaluate information found on various Web sites since some are presented as factual evidence but offer inaccurate and unreliable sources. It is critical that you carefully evaluate documents before relying on them in your research. Since it is impossible to avoid it, we must learn how to evaluate the millions of Web sites that are posted there. A major weakness of publishing on the Web is that almost anyone can post information, whether it is correct or not, without the editorial scrutiny that the material would typically undergo if it were being published in hard copy. Students also refer to Web sites in writing a paper for class, and scholars also refer to them as legitimate sources or for literature review.

Some of the basic questions you need to ask before you rely on them are (Harnack et al. 2001): (1) Whose Web site is it? (2) Is it a reputable individual's site? (3) Is the material dated or when was it last updated? (4) Does the Web site present primary source material or just secondary source material? (5) Can the information be corroborated? (6) Are complete references to cited material given?

For example, the use of Wikipedia, a free encyclopedia started in 2001, has been much debated in recent years. It is an online dictionary written and edited by anyone who claims to be an expert. How reliable is Wikipedia? To what extent it can be used in research is debatable. By August 2009, the English Wikipedia had published 3 million articles; there are currently Wikipedias in more than 280 languages. The encyclopedia is among the top 10 most-visited sites on the Internet around the world, aided by the fact that Google searches typically list Wikipedia entries prominently on results pages. The company announced in August 2009 that it began to impose editorial review on articles on living people (Cohen 2009).

Advantages of the Web sites are that Web sources are often more up-to-date than conventionally printed professional journals. You are encouraged to use more general Web sources for retrieving information from the Web. Similarly, the strength of the Web is that its quick changeability and content flexibility allows individuals and organizations to promptly post current information. Prior to the development of the Web, the dissemination of information often had a publication lag of up to a year in traditional, hard-copy publishing. It was not uncommon for a printed journal article or book to be published a year or more after it was written.

As the Web becomes an essential source of information for those who research, it is important to establish criteria to consider when evaluating a Web-based source of information. Consider accessing information posted on the Web by professional associations since various organizations post information as well as statistical data on the Internet.

PLAGIARISM

The advent of the Internet made plagiarism extremely easy. Students must understand the importance of citations and references. Some do not understand the gravity of plagiarism. When you lift an idea, a sentence, or a passage from someone's writing without citing the sources, it is called plagiarism. According to Merriam-Webster's Online Dictionary (www.merriam-webster.com), "to plagiarize" is "to steal and pass off the ideas or words of another as one's own; use another's production without crediting the source." Failure to cite a source for an original idea constitutes plagiarism even if the idea or point of view is logical and makes common sense.

ETHICAL ISSUES AND THE INSTITUTIONAL REVIEW BOARD (IRB)

All social research should be carried out in ways designed to avoid any physical or psychological risks to those involved, such as participants, respondents, and interviewers. Procedures need to be ethically managed since social scientific research deals with human subjects. The researcher should make sure that no individual in the research suffers any adverse consequences as a result of the research while maximizing positive outcomes of the research process. The research process generally involves enlisting voluntary cooperation. For instance, it is a basic premise of ethical survey research that respondents should be informed about what it is that they are volunteering for.

In 1974 the National Research Act was passed by Congress, and the National Commission on Protection of Human Subjects of Biomedical and Behavioral Research was created by Title II of this law (Lane 2009). The National Research Act directed all institutions that sponsored research to establish institutional review committees, today more commonly called Institutional Review Boards (IRBs). Locally based in-house IRBs were now charged with the responsibility of carefully reviewing any proposed research that involved human subjects (Lane 2009). IRBs were expected to ensure that researchers had considered potential risks and benefits to subjects, that important scientific knowledge could be derived from the project, that legally informed consent would be obtained from each subject, and that the rights and interests of subjects were protected. IRB review is designed to protect subjects, researchers, and institutions (Fowler 2002: 147).

Almost all universities and most other organizations in the United States that conduct federally funded research have an Institutional Review Board (IRB) that is responsible for overseeing, evaluating, and reviewing research projects. They have formal review procedures for student and faculty research projects with human subjects. If a review panel is concerned about possible harm to subjects, an informed consent document may be required. The signed document would help assure that subjects fully understood the extent and possible consequences of their involvement in the research process. Therefore, when research is proposed, the main researcher, if it is a group research, must submit the proposed protocol for IRB review before beginning to collect data.

CONCLUSION

Once a researcher understands the whole research process, it makes the process easier and more efficient during the preparation stage. Each step of the process needs to be carefully examined, from the formulation of a research question, the selection of research methods to the final data collection and conclusion. None of the steps can be excluded or eliminated from the process. Human begins have subjective viewpoints in their everyday life, but we must learn to have an objective standpoint when we are conducting social scientific research although we know that there is a subjective interest in fashion/dress based on our personal values and experiences.

GUIDE TO FURTHER READING

Babbie, Earl (1998), *The Practice of Social Research,* Belmont, CA: Wadsworth Publishing.

Bordens, Kenneth, and Bruce Barrington Abbott (2007), *Research Design and Methods: A Process Approach,* New York: McGraw-Hill.

Flick, Uwe (1998), *An Introduction to Qualitative Research,* Newbury Park, CA: Sage Publications.

Harnack, Andrew, Eugene Kleppinger, and Gene Kleppinger (2001), *Online!: A Reference Guide to Using Internet Sources,* New York: Bedford/St. Martin's.

Lane, Eliesh O'Neil (2009), *Institutional Review Boards: Decision-making in Human Subject Research,* Saarbrücken, Germany: VDM Verlag.

Maner, Martin (1999), *The Research Process: A Complete Guide and Reference for Writers,* New York: McGraw-Hill.

Marshall, Catherine, and Gretchen B. Rossman (1999), *Designing Qualitative Research,* Newbury Park, CA: Sage Publications.

Mills, C. Wright (2000 [1959]), *The Sociological Imagination,* Oxford, UK: Oxford University Press.

Muggleton, David (2000), *Inside Subculture: The Postmodern Meaning of Style,* Oxford, UK: Berg.

Weber, Max (1949), *The Methodology of the Social Sciences,* New York: Free Press.

3 ETHNOGRAPHY

Objectives

■ To understand what ethnography means and its brief history.

■ To learn the differences and similarities between sociological ethnography and anthropological ethnography.

■ To explore the process of ethnography.

■ To examine the role of a researcher as an insider and an outsider.

■ To learn how to conduct observation/participant observation/listening.

■ To understand the role played by an informant/research collaborator.

■ To make an analysis of ethnographical data.

■ To recognize the strengths and weaknesses of ethnography.

■ To review specific ethnographical studies.

Ethnography is a qualitative, descriptive, nonmathematical, naturalistic way to study human beings, their life and their behavior, including the way they dress, in their own natural settings. Ethnography tells a story about a group of people, but it is also a process, that is, the method of inquiry. It is an investigation process that social scientists, mainly qualitative sociologists and cultural anthropologists, employ in different ways to study how human beings act and why they act in the way they do.

Ethnography includes participant and nonparticipant observation in addition to listening and interviewing. These methods are used to acquire firsthand experience as well as accounts of phenomena as they occur in natural real-life situations, and there are no prior manipulations or control of variables in the study as we find in experiments. A researcher has or imposes no control over what he or she sees or hears. The only choice he or she has is where/which location and who to study. The task of ethnographers is to reconstruct the characteristics of the phenomenon they observe. This method reveals research subjects' own perspectives, which may be useful for developing new theories. But findings are usually relevant to one particular case and are not generalizable to other cases or useful for testing theories.

In addition to Malinowski's pioneering ethnographical study (2008 [1922]), we have much to learn from Geertz's seminal work on *The Interpretations of Cultures* (1973), in which he makes it clear that the concept of culture is inseparable from ethnography, particularly for anthropologists. According to Geertz (1973: 5–6), in anthropology, what the practitioners do is ethnography, and it is in understanding what ethnography is, or more exactly what doing ethnography is, that a start can be made toward grasping what anthropological analysis amounts to as a form of knowledge. Ethnography is "thick description" (Geertz 1973: 9–10). It is not only the cultural anthropologists who use ethnography but also qualitative sociologists.

Many social scientists, anthropologists, and sociologists in particular (Dalby 1983, 1998; Eicher 1998; Hamilton and Hamilton 2008; Janowski 1998; Tarlo 1996; Wilkie 1998), use the method to study how people dress in a particular culture and to explore the cultural meaning and symbolism of their dress. In this chapter, in addition to Joanne Eicher's ethnographical studies on Nigerian beads and beadmakers (1998), Dalby's work on Japanese kimono (1998), Tarlo's study in a Gujarati village (1996), and Hodkinson's study on Goth subculture in the United Kingdom (2002) are discussed as examples.

It is a useful method in studying fashion/dress because every cultural object or artifact situates itself within a particular domain. You cannot simply study dress because dress is situated within a cultural context, and the two are inseparable. Dalby's study on kimono (1998) derives from her ethnographical work as geisha during 1973–1976. Geisha are kimono experts and professional kimono wearers. Dalby wore kimono every day during her fieldwork and writes: "Inevitably anthropologists become interested in the things that interest the people they work with. Geisha are interested in kimono. Their wardrobe is their biggest professional expense, but geisha don't add to their brimming cedar chests just because they have to—they long to" (Dalby 1998: 6). She explores political hierarchy, the aesthetics of color, the sociology of gender, and the logic of formal systems while studying about kimono.

Some researchers have found that very long-term participant observation, done in a series of studies over several decades, can yield understanding of social change that is simply not possible in any other way. However, most basic ethnographical research is done over a period of about a year or two.

Ethnographic and qualitative research is often equated with hermeneutic[1] or interpretive research, though not all hermeneutic or interpretive studies are ethnographies. A concern with hermeneutics involves a concern with meaning, and it is concerned with ways to explain, translate, and interpret perceived reality. In contemporary research, a concern with hermeneutics is a concern for interpreting and recounting accurately the meanings that research participants give to the reality around them.

A BRIEF HISTORY OF ETHNOGRAPHY

Franz Boaz (1858–1942) was not the first to systematically study culture nor was he America's first ethnographer. But he is considered the father of fieldwork in American cultural anthropology. He was the first to professionalize the discipline, introduce an inductive analysis of culture, and instill ethnographic fieldwork as its principal research method. He trained the first generation of American anthropologists at Columbia University such as Alfred Kroeber, Margaret Mead, Edward Sapir, and Ruth Benedict,[2] among others, some of whom have written about fashion and dress. What they had done can be applicable to any research using the ethnographical method.

Boaz was not particularly clear about the practice and process of fieldwork. It was the Polish expatriate Bronislaw Malinowski (1884–1942) who advanced the methodology of ethnographic investigation through his research among the Trobrianders of Melanesia. Malinowski influenced the twentieth-century ethnographical research methods and was the first anthropologist to describe what intensive fieldwork was like and what it entailed. He gathered data by living with the Trobriand people and observed their everyday activities. His book *Argonauts of the Western Pacific* published in 1922 is widely read and is most influential to those who use ethnography as a research method. According to Malinowski (1922: 3), all ethnographic studies should include an account of the research methods and conditions so that at a glance the reader could estimate with precision the degree of the writer's personal acquaintance with the facts that he or she describes and form an idea under what conditions information had been obtained from the natives.

During the 1920s and 1930s, sociologists at the University of Chicago, influenced by the work of social psychologist George Herbert Mead, exerted an influence on the development of sociology and anthropology. As indicated in Chapter 1, "Theory and Practice," they came to be known as the Chicago School and were led by Herbert Blumer,[3] William Thomas, Robert Park, and Charles Horton Cooley. They represented the first major attempt to conduct systematic ethnographic fieldwork in sociology in particular. They encouraged their students to conduct fieldwork and reconceptualized their methodology around "participant observation," which was originally developed by Malinowski.

In order to conduct a successful ethnographical study, there needs to be physical proximity of the fieldworker to the people studied, knowledge of their language, and a high degree of psychological and emotional involvement while maintaining the objective standpoint of a researcher as discussed in Chapter 2, "Research Process." You need to be totally involved and yet observe with complete detachment, continuously to step in and out of other cultures. Much ethnographic research involves entering the setting of some group and simply watching and listening attentively.

Since it would be impossible to observe everything or hear all that is going on at one time, ethnographers must watch and listen only to certain portions of what happens. Therefore, you need to determine exactly what you as a researcher want to learn about at various points in the research.

SOCIOLOGICAL ETHNOGRAPHY VERSUS ANTHROPOLOGICAL ETHNOGRAPHY

According to Geertz (1973: 5), cultural analysis is not an experimental science in search of law but an interpretive one in search of meaning. Ethnography offers approaches for analyzing clothing and body ornament that stem from the study of the technological and cultural roots of specific peasant and small-scale communities (Taylor 2002a: 193), and this is an anthropological understanding of ethnography that plays an important role in methods in understanding culture.

Ethnography as a method is associated with a group of theoretical perspectives from sociology and anthropology, such as structural functionalism, symbolic interactionism, social exchange theory, and conflict theory. More recent scholars also employ critical, feminist, and poststructural approaches to their research. The outcome of ethnography is tied to theory. But it is most often associated with cultural anthropology and qualitative sociology. While ethnography is practiced by cultural anthropologists as well as sociologists, sociologists differ on the conceptual meaning of ethnography and its application. In an attempt to differentiate this style of research from anthropological ethnography, many sociologists have called their ethnography "street ethnography" or "urban ethnography." The direct observation of the activity of members of a particular social group, and the description and evaluation of such activity, constitute ethnography. Various sociologists (Hodkinson 2002; Kawamura 2004; Manlow 2007; Muggleton 2000) have also used ethnography as a method of inquiry to investigate a fashion phenomenon, and it is also used to study the contemporary fashion environment.

Whichever ethnography it is, ethnography is that the practice places researchers in the midst of whatever it is that they study. In this way, they can examine various phenomena as perceived by participants and represent these observations as accounts. Traditionally speaking, cultural anthropologists study non-Western cultures while sociologists study Western, industrialized cultures. However, these distinctions are becoming increasingly blurry in an age where scholars work beyond their disciplines and are interdisciplinary. In the areas of fashion and dress, those who use ethnography as a method study not only non-Western societies but also Western societies. Therefore, the method of ethnography can be adopted in studying Western or non-Western fashion/dress.

PREPARING FOR ETHNOGRAPHY

Once you decide where your ethnography is going to take place, you must gain access to the place. Gaining entry into a site/community is the very first step of ethnography. But in ethnography, there is always a problem of getting entry into a group that you are studying. This involves consideration of who the subjects are and the nature of the setting.

Prior knowledge and acquiring information about a culture that you are getting into obviously is a major advantage since you can be ready for incidents that are familiar to you. Knowing the people's customs, traditions, norms, and beliefs facilitates you to the entry. The first step begins in the library, and you need to locate as much information as possible about the culture before you actually go to the field. A referral is also important in some cultures and communities. Formal and informal social networks are useful in reaching research subjects. Occasionally, there are gatekeepers that you may first need to introduce yourself to. You also need some luck and to take advantage of certain relationships while conducting considerable background work; making the right contacts can also allow you to get access to restricted groups.

Manlow, who conducted an ethnographical study at a fashion house in New York, writes: "I wrote to about one hundred firms—many well-known and others less so. I heard from two firms: Leslie Faye and Tommy Hilfiger" (2007: vii). Manlow conducted a participant observation at Tommy Hilfiger with full access. She was set up as an intern with an employee identification card, an e-mail account, a desk, and a computer. She was given insider privilege. Like many other sociologists who study fashion (Aspers 2006; Entwistle 2006, 2009; Kawamura 2004, 2006; Skov 2006), she is not concerned about the actual raw materials of clothes but is interested in how the fashion design process is organized, what kind of organization culture exists, and how Hilfiger and others manage the firm. Manlow interviewed designers in other fashion firms and also obtained secondary data from various sources (2007: viii). The names of those interviewed are often changed to protect their privacy. In her study, Manlow mentions Hilfiger himself, but other names have been changed.

How ethnographers gain entry into their research settings varies from individual to individual, from place to place, and from culture to culture. Some people are more accepting than others, and some communities are more welcoming and easier to enter than others. In contrast, there are those who are more suspicious of outsiders and are reluctant to accept strangers. Unless you as the ethnographer are accepted to a certain extent, you would not be able to conduct any ethnographical research.

In conducting an ethnographical study on male fashion modeling and fashion buying, Entwistle writes that she failed to gain access to photo shoots that are notoriously difficult to get inside (Entwistle 2009: 4). Access must be negotiated and renegotiated throughout the research process, and it is based on sets of relationship between the researcher and the researched throughout the project.

THE RESEARCHER AS AN INSIDER VERSUS AN OUTSIDER

Depending on the research topic and site, you as the ethnographer may be partially an insider to the community you are involved in or you may have started as an outsider like Dalby (1993) and then become almost an insider. There are advantages and disadvantages in both.

Tarlo (1996) conducted an ethnographical study in a Gujarati village in India to research the culture and its dress. The members of one family that she met were friendly since it was through their youngest son who studied in the city that Tarlo and her colleagues made their initial contact. Tarlo struggles to find out how she should be dressed or what is the most appropriate way of dress among them. She explains her anxiety as follows:

> the feeling of exclusion and peculiarity engendered by being inappropriately dressed, and the feeling of group inclusion with all the apparent limitations and restrictions for a garment sufficiently neutral to allow me to circulate among the maximum number of people, decent without being confining, female without being too "feminine," and Indian without being associated with any particular caste. (Tarlo 1996: 133)

She eventually chose the white shalwar kamiz that was shapeless, de-emphasized the female body and wore no jewelry. The family that she was staying with wanted her to eat their food, wear their clothes, and to be one of them, that is, become a complete insider. She writes (1996: 132): "I realized that 'being one of them' was going to place insurmountable restrictions on my movements. I had already seen that unmarried Brahman daughters scarcely stirred outside the house."

Since you are immersed in their culture, limitations may occur, and that can become an obstacle to your ethnography. In Tarlo's case, it was a cause of great concern that an unmarried girl could stray so far afield without her parents, and it also seemed inconceivable that any university could allow such irresponsible behavior. She writes (1996: 132): "Ideally, a respectable girl of marriageable age should stay inside the house as much as possible, and if my studies took me outside I should at least be accompanied by a male family member." For the first few days of her stay, she was accompanied by her Gujarati brother when she went to talk to the farming women and girls. Tarlo later managed to gain her identity as the friend and neighbor of their relative who lives in a foreign country, and her position and role as a partial insider and a partial outsider made her study effective.

THE DIFFICULTY OF OBJECTIVITY IN ETHNOGRAPHY

Although the importance of objectivity is stressed repeatedly in social sciences, ethnography as a research method requires a researcher to immerse himself or herself into the field with the awareness of objectivity. In ethnography, there is always the danger of "going native," which is considered to be one of the few taboos in the area. It means that you are completely immersed into their culture. It used to be a criticism to go native, but in the postmodern era, those who take on the postmodern[4] critique of empiricism and objectivity advocate the breakdown of the traditional barrier between the observer and the observed. Some researchers describe the ethnographic process as subjective and not objective, and the researcher may have to compromise objectivity slightly. In ethnography, you are not simply looking at mathematical data and making a statistical analysis. You are interacting on a daily basis with human beings who have emotions and feelings.

Therefore, in participant observation, objectivity is often said to be difficult to maintain, although researchers are well aware of its importance and meaning. Dalby conducted research on Japanese culture, geisha, and kimono. She went to Japan and lived with geisha. She interviewed geisha, ex-geisha, the owners of geisha houses, and registry office officials in fourteen geisha communities during the fourteen months of her study (1983: xiv). Dalby managed to get access to a secret world of geisha to conduct her ethnographical fieldwork. She conducted participant observation, took a name, *Ichiguku,* as all the other geisha girls do, and attended parties and events with professional geisha girls. Dalby writes:

> I tried to be a perceptive observer of all that went on; yet I soon found that I had plunged my whole heart into the endeavor and could not maintain the conventional researcher's separation from the object of study. I was absorbed in learning to be a geisha. The objectivity, the sorting of my experience, and the analysis came much later. (Dalby 1983: xv)

Thus, she makes an attempt to integrate the two viewpoints, that of an outsider and an insider, as a geisha. She explains that her study is not simply an ethnography but an interpretive ethnography that explains the cultural meaning of persons, objects, and situations in the geisha world. She intentionally writes her book in the first person, which is unique in a research-based publication.

Geertz is one of the scholars who insists on the importance of a researcher being a complete insider. To look at the symbolic dimensions of social action—art, religion, ideology, science, law, morality, common sense—is not to turn away from the existential dilemmas of life for some empyrean realm of de-emotionalized forms; it is to plunge into the midst of them (Geertz 1973: 30).

The researcher must be aware that he or she is part of the social world that he or she is investigating. It requires the researcher to avoid simply accepting everything at face value. Ethnography is a process of gathering systematic observations, partly through participation and partly through various types of conversational interviews, along with photography, archival searches, and assorted documents. The long-term immersion in foreign societies and cultures or unfamiliar communities and the status as a foreigner and an outsider using interactive research methods have far-reaching effects on the self as well as the perspectives on others. The researcher's identity has a decisive influence on the data gathered, which may compromise objectivity, one of the key factors in social sciences.

HAWTHORNE EFFECT

One of the obstacles in conducting ethnographic research is the very presence of the ethnographer in the field. When the research subject becomes aware of the presence of an ethnographer, he or she may change his or her behavior, and it may no longer be his or her everyday routine behavior or comments. This is called the Hawthorne effect.[5] Ethnography should occur within a natural setting with a natural behavior from those you are studying. This effect is usually short-lived, but the presence of ethnographers in a social setting might certainly reactivate the Hawthorne effect in various degrees every time someone new is introduced to the researchers. Ethnographers must be invisible and must try to be invisible. The status as an invisible researcher is the ability to be present in the setting, to see what is going on without being observed, and consequently to capture the essence of the setting and participants without influencing them. For instance, if a person who usually wears a T-shirt and a pair of jeans suddenly dresses up after finding out that she is being studied, ethnography can no longer be conducted in that situation.

However, participant observation is believed to reduce the problem of reactivity, that is, people changing their behavior when they know that they are being studied. Lower reactivity means higher validity of data. It also gives you an intuitive understanding of what is going on in a culture and allows you to speak with confidence about the meaning of data. It also allows you to make strong statements about cultural facts you collect. There are things that you cannot obtain from a survey or a questionnaire. Participant observation makes it possible to collect both quantitative survey data and qualitative interview data from a representative sample of a population.

OBSERVATION/PARTICIPANT OBSERVATION/ LISTENING

Geertz borrows the term "thick description" from Gilbert Ryle and says that doing ethnography is establishing rapport, selecting informants, transcribing texts, taking genealogies, mapping fields, keeping a diary, and so on. But it is not these things, techniques, and received procedures that define the enterprise. What defines it is the kind of intellectual effort it is: an elaborate venture in, to borrow a notion from Gilbert Ryle, "thick description" (Geertz 1973: 6) in contrast to "thin description."

Fieldwork involves both observation and participant observation. This may appear to be such a simplistic way to research, but observation as a method is not as easy as one may think it is. It requires a deep insight into what you are studying. You become a human wall with your eyes and ears wide open. In participant observation, you are not simply observing but you are also participating and getting involved with those you are studying.

> What the ethnographer is in fact faced with is complex conceptual structures, many of them superimposed upon or knotted into one another, which are at once strange, irregular and inexplicit, and which he must contrive somehow first to grasp and then to render. . . . Those who employ ethnography as a method of inquiry untangle the knotted web to understand what a culture consists of. Doing ethnography is like trying to read a foreign, faded, incoherent manuscript. (Geertz 1973: 10)

For instance, Eicher (1998) examines the significance of textiles and beads in Kalabari life through her fieldwork in Nigeria. She observes a final funeral dance in 1983 and studies what dancers wear. Field observations, photographs, and field notes from eight fieldtrips were made between 1980–1996, and she explains that hats and girdles decorated with glass beads are an exclusive possession of the Fubara family worn primarily by women at funeral celebrations. Eicher (1998) also examines the labor conditions of the women who make, thread, or work with beads and analyzes their activities as traders, entrepreneurs, and employers of other women. From the making process to the exchange, she explores the uses and the symbolic meanings of beads in the study.

Adler and Adler explain what an ethnographer should and should not do:

> Observers neither stimulate nor manipulate their subjects. They do not ask the subjects research questions, pose tasks for them, or deliberately create new provocations. This stands in marked contrast to researchers using interview questionnaires, who direct the interaction and introduce potentially new ideas into the arena, and to experimental researchers, who often set up

structured situations where they can alter certain conditions to measure the covariance of others. (Adler and Adler 1998: 80)

An ethnographer is an objective observer while placing himself or herself among the insiders. Physically, he or she is in, but emotionally, he or she is detached, but that separation in one's mind is sometimes difficult to maintain because mind and body are connected as one.

GETTING USED TO SURROUNDINGS

When ethnographers arrive at a new place, they usually wander around the location they plan to use as the research setting. Then they begin to map the setting carefully. You decide where to cover and how to cover in the most efficient and effective way, such as the number of hours required each day for the study, which days or which hours during the day or night are the best. By wandering around, you also get acquainted with inhabitants and they get used to having you around also. You may get first impressions that may not be accurate in the beginning but can be used as points of reference later on in the research process.

DEVELOPING RELATIONSHIPS

This process is part of gaining entry into your research area and community. Participant observation is the foundation of ethnographical research. It involves establishing rapport in a new culture and a community, learning to act so that people go about their business as usual when you are there, and removing yourself every day from cultural immersion so you can objectively observe what you are seeing and hearing. Smiling and greeting in the beginning may help you get acquainted with the locals and finding guides and informants. It is not a good idea to elaborate on technical details of the study. It is not necessary nor are they interested in knowing all the details of your research. Who you are and what you are doing should be enough information to give them. A brief response is enough. The most important thing is to gain their trust and minimize their anxiety when you approach them. You can also tell them that all information collected during the research study will be kept confidential. Once you build a rapport with a guide or informant, you can begin snowballing additional relationships with other inhabitants.

TRACKING, OBSERVING, LISTENING, AND ASKING QUESTIONS

After you establish relationships with several guides and inhabitants, you are free to begin learning what goes on among the inhabitants of the study domain. Tracking literally means following the guides around during their usual daily routines and watching their activities and the other people they interact with. As you follow and observe, you can also eavesdrop on conversations. You can ask questions but must take a passive role during informal questioning. Jotting down some points to ask at a later time would serve better than interrupting the ongoing action with a question.

INTERVIEWING

This can also be used in ethnographical study to supplement observation and participant observation. While structured and semi-structured interviews are used in surveys as discussed in Chapter 4, "Survey Methods," unstructured interviews are used in ethnography. They are completely unstructured, no fixed order or wording to any questions. Any type of language can be used. The interviewer may answer questions and make clarifications, and the interviewer may add or delete questions between interviews. This is used during the course of fieldwork to expand field observations. Unstructured interviews allow researchers to acquire additional information about various phenomena they may observe by asking questions. It can provide important information for these investigators along with the data gathered from various published and unpublished articles and documents.

TAKING NOTES

The central component of ethnographic research is the ethnographic account. Providing such narrative accounts of what goes on in the lives of research subjects derives from having maintained complete, accurate, and detailed field notes. Field notes should be completed immediately following every excursion into the field, as well as following any chance meeting with inhabitants outside the boundaries of the study setting, because human memories can fade away rather quickly. There are variations about how to take field notes. Some researchers wait until they have left the field and then immediately write complete records. Others take abbreviated notes covertly while in the field and later translate them into complete field notes. Field notes usually include the date, time, and place of the observations; specific facts, numbers, and details of what happened at the site; sensory impressions such as sights, sounds, textures, smells, tastes. Personal responses are also recorded in the field notes. Specific words, phrases, summaries of conversations, and questions about people or behaviors at the site for future consideration are also noted.

There are various ways to take field notes. For example, some ethnographers carry tape recorders and periodically enter their own notes or record various conversations they witness. Others carry a notepad or index cards and simply jot down notes or verbatim quotes periodically throughout the field excursion. Once out of the field, the researchers can use these notes and jotted points to write full accounts.

THE ROLE OF AN INFORMANT/RESEARCH COLLABORATOR

Informants (some prefer to call them research collaborators) play a crucial role in ethnography. They are the insiders or the locals of the group being studied and are involved in everyday activities. Through the informant, your network could begin to snowball as he or she would introduce you to others in the community. The informant must be convinced that the ethnographers are who they claim to be and that the study is meaningful. The larger the ethnographers' network of reliable informants, the greater their access and ability to gain further cooperation. The informant can introduce the ethnographers to people in the group that they may have less access to.

Aspers in his study explained the importance of an informant in studying the fashion photography market in Sweden as follows:

> As I began the project I knew relatively little about the market for fashion photography, my research agenda was diffuse, and the study did not have a clear focus. At this stage informants proved to be especially important. They gave me information I might not have asked for otherwise, and ideas on what to study and how to do so. Simply by talking to them I got a lot of ideas, and further questions arose. (Aspers 2001: 39)

Aspers had three photographers, three of their assistants, and one stylist as his informants who provided him with valuable information. He learned things that he could not have imagined simply from reading, such as the enormous amount of unpaid work done by the actors.

Informants are often the insiders to the community or the group the researcher wants to study so they obviously have more inside information than the researcher who is considered an outsider and therefore, has limited or no access whatsoever to unreleased or confidential information.

MAKING AN ANALYSIS OF ETHNOGRAPHICAL DATA

The basic goal of ethnography is to create a vivid reconstruction of the culture or the community being studied. This requires researchers first to separate, for analytics purposes, any empirical, unbiased meanings they have assigned to behavior and belief from meanings assigned to the same behaviors and beliefs by their participants. Researcher-constructed descriptions of reality may be quite different from the meanings that participants use to construct their reality. Realities are socially constructed and are different for everyone (Berger and Luckmann 1966). Ethnographers are concerned with interpreting events and people's behavior accurately, but because they can only see some portions of a cultural and social reality, they struggle with the issue of portrayal. Many ethnographers believe that the reality of a cultural or a social scene is the product of multiple perceptions, including that of the researcher and that produced by the interaction between researchers and the people they study. The problem becomes one of determining how much of whose reality is depicted, how it can be portrayed, and with what degree of adequacy (Geertz and Marcus 1986).

At this stage, it is time to reread the data you collected. Check the data for completeness and reacquaint the research with territory previously covered. Researchers who postpone analysis until data collection is complete should scan their records before leaving the field so that critical gaps left accidentally in the collecting or recording of data may be remedied. You may become too familiar with certain events and neglect to document them thoroughly. You tend to omit the subtleties that you take for granted. Then you later find out that you have left out some valuable information and evidence. Data collection and data analysis must occur almost at the same time (Hamilton and Hamilton 2008).

Next you create an outline from your notes. The outline begins with a search for regularities, that is, things that happen frequently with groups of people. Patterns and regularities are transformed into categories into which subsequent items are sorted. These categories or patterns are discovered from the data. They emerge in a rather systematic, if not totally conscious, application of the processes, and this could potentially lead to building a new theory.

HODKINSON'S ETHNOGRAPHICAL STUDY OF GOTH SUBCULTURE IN THE UNITED KINGDOM

Hodkinson (2002) conducted in-depth qualitative research on the Goth scene in Britain for a number of years. His research goal was to focus on the norms, meanings, motivations, and social patterns of those involved as well as the voluntary and commercial events, media, and consumables that appeared to enable the Goth scene to exist and survive on such a small scale (2002: 4). He combined various qualitative methods, such as participant observation, in-depth interviews, media analysis, and a questionnaire. There are several interesting ethnographical studies on Goth, but Hodkinson's study best articulates the research process and methodologies that many researchers tend not to explain clearly in their work.

Hodkinson himself is part of the Goth subculture. Therefore, he is completely an insider. He explains the transition in Chapter 1, "From Participant to Researcher," of his book. He knows how he should dress, which music to listen to, which magazines and novels to read to be part of the subculture. He writes: "Although the style is diverse and somewhat malleable, goths rarely find it difficult to identify one another through appearance" (Hodkinson 2002: 2). Unlike Dalby who is not exactly a geisha but pretends to be and acts like a geisha in her research, Hodkinson is a true insider to the group he studies.

Hodkinson (2002: 4) writes: "I had been an enthusiastic participant in the goth scene since the beginning of that decade (1990s), but in 1996, my personal involvement became just one part of an extensive research project." He is in "an unambiguous position as a long-term genuine participant of the goth scene" (2002: 4). But the role of researcher should take a different viewpoint from that of an insider. He explains his complex status in his research as follows:

> Indeed, in some respects my insider status was actually enhanced, as the project was built around an intensified attendance of clubs, gigs and festivals across Britain, including a concentrated focus on the cities of Birmingham, Plymouth and Leeds. Participation on internet discussion groups and other goth internet facilities widened the scope of my research within Britain, and was the main source of my more limited information and contacts outside the country. Whether off- or on-line, the authenticity of my participation greatly enhanced the process of acquiring contacts, interviewees and information. As well as having a suitable appearance, the manner in which I behaved in clubs—dancing, requesting songs from DJs and socializing—made meeting people, arranging interviews, taking photographs and gaining advice far easier than they might otherwise have been. (Hodkinson 2002: 5)

Subjective experience and meanings required critical interpretation of research aims and theory and were complemented by more distanced forms of observation and analysis (Hodkinson 2002: 6), and thus it requires a researcher to take a few steps back so that he can critically and objectively evaluate and assess the outcome of the research. In an interview setting, Hodkinson's insider status also made it easier for his interviewees to express themselves openly. He interviewed a total of seventy-two individuals (DJs, event promoters, fanzine editors, bands, record label proprietors, and specialist retailers) in fifty-six separate open-ended interviews. With a few exceptions of those interviewed by mail and e-mail, the interviews were conducted face-to-face.

HAMILTON AND HAMILTON'S ETHNOGRAPHICAL STUDY OF THE THAI KAREN DRESS

Ethnography is the most popular method in researching ethnic dress. Hamilton and Hamilton's study (2008) on the dress that a group of hill tribe people known as the Karen wears is a classic example of such a study. They clearly indicate the methods that they used and how their research was executed. Through observation and participant observation, their collected data includes original field notes, slides and photographs, and material artifacts. They explain their data collection method as follows:

> The techniques of data collection can include, but are not necessarily limited to, structured and unstructured interviews, life histories, solicited and unsolicited conversations, involvement and experience with the daily and seasonal round of activity, unobtrusive observation of ongoing behavior and interaction, and observation on the production and use of material culture. (Hamilton and Hamilton 2008: 142)

If you are only looking at a dress that the Karen women wore without any prior knowledge, you have no idea what the dress symbolizes and represents. By observing those who are wearing the dress, the way they interact, communicate, and socialize with other men, women, and children, do we understand what the dress means to them and what they represent in their culture. Ethnography plays a crucial role in such a study.

Hamilton and Hamilton's ethnographic data was collected by one of the authors during nearly two years of fieldwork on-site in a Karen tribal village in northwest Thailand. Nearly two years of fieldwork was broken into two periods: (1) seventeen months, and (2) six months ten years after the first study.

The author explains the initial preparation in and the techniques for getting access to the community he wishes to study as follows. Prior to the onset of fieldwork, the researcher spent five months in Bangkok in intensive study of the Thai language, cultivation of governmental sanctions for the study, and the evaluation of potential community sites for the study. Once the research was in the field, he lived for ten months in a Thai village two miles from the Karen village and commuted every day by bicycle. A Karen-Thai translator was hired until the Karen language was sufficiently mastered and the translator was no longer needed. Knowing their native language was a big advantage in conducting ethnography in a foreign culture where people do not speak English.

> At the end of the ten-month period, he had earned enough trust in the Karen village and propitiated the village spirits sufficiently that he was allowed to move into the Karen village and build a house there. Eventually he was ceremonially adopted as the son of the village head elder. (Hamilton and Hamilton 2008: 143)

Ethnography is a time-consuming method, but research on ethnic dress requires such a methodological strategy. In order for us to study unknown and unfamiliar cultural objects, such as the Thai Karen dress, we must understand that this is about the only way to study it since there is hardly any existing written documents or literature on the topic in English.

CONCLUSION

Ethnography involves extensive fieldwork of various types including observation, participant observation, formal and informal interviewing, document collecting, filming and recording, among others. It is a process that attempts to describe and interpret social expressions between people and groups. We examine the context and nature of the interactions between them. The purpose of the descriptive research is to document exactly what happened. A collection of empirical data that generates complete descriptions of events, interactions, and activities leads logically and immediately into the development or application of categories and relationships that allow interpretation of that data. Why and how people dress in what situations can only be accurately explained through ethnographical research.

GUIDE TO FURTHER READING

Aspers, Patrik (2001), *Markets in Fashion: A Phenomenological Approach,* Stockholm, Sweden: City University Press.

Csikszentmihalyi, Mihaly, and Eugene Rochberg-Halton (1981), *The Meaning of Things: Domestic Symbols and the Self,* Cambridge, UK: Cambridge University Press.

Dalby, Liza (1983), *Geisha,* Berkeley: University of California Press.

Dalby, Liza (1998), *Kimono: Fashioning Culture,* New Haven, CT: Yale University Press.

Eicher, Joanne B. (1998), "Beaded and Bedecked Kalabari of Nigeria," in Lidia D. Sciama and Joanne B. Eicher (eds.), *Beads and Bead Makers: Gender, Material Culture and Meaning,* pp. 95–116, Oxford, UK: Berg.

Geertz, Clifford (1973), *The Interpretation of Cultures,* New York: Basic Books.

Hamilton, Jean A., and Hamilton, James W. (2008), "Dress as a Reflection and Sustainer of Social Reality: A Cross-Cultural Perspective," in Joanne B. Eicher, Sandra Lee Evenson, and Hazel A. Lutz (eds.), *The Visible Self: Global Perspectives on Dress, Culture, and Society,* pp. 141–9, New York: Fairchild Publications.

Hodkinson, Paul (2002), *Goth, Identity, Style and Subculture,* Oxford, UK: Berg.

Malinowski, Bronislaw (2008 [1922]), *Argonauts of the Western Pacific: An Account of Native Enterprise and Adventure in the Archipelagoes of Melanesian New Guinea,* Whitefish, MT: Kessinger Publishing.

Manlow, Veronica (2007), *Designing Clothes: Culture and Organization of the Fashion Industry,* New Brunswick, NJ: Transaction Publishers.

Meisch, Lynn A. (1998), "'Why Do They Like Red?' Beads, Ethnicity and Gender in Ecuador," in Lidia D. Sciama and Joanne B. Eicher (eds.), *Beads and Bead Makers: Gender, Material Culture and Meaning,* pp. 147–75, Oxford, UK: Berg.

Sciama, Lidia D., and Eicher, Joanne B. (eds.) (1998), *Beads and Bead Makers: Gender, Material Culture and Meaning,* Oxford, UK: Berg.

Tarlo, Emma (1996), *Clothing Matters: Dress and Identity in India,* Chicago: University of Chicago Press.

4 SURVEY METHODS

Objectives

■ To understand what a survey method is and what it consists of.

■ To learn how to create a questionnaire.

■ To learn how to conduct an interview.

■ To examine how to choose a research sampling, to create a focus group and case studies.

■ To recognize the importance of preparing graphs and tables using graphics software.

■ To distinguish structured interviews from semi-structured interviews.

■ To review specific studies using survey methods.

Almost everyone at least a couple of times in his or her lifetime must have answered surveys. Similar to ethnography discussed in the previous chapter, it is an obtrusive measure. Some of the answers in the survey method are converted into numbers and become quantitative. But in this chapter, I discuss the process before the statistical manipulation and after the statistical results are generated by professional statisticians, and I also cover some aspects of a survey method, such as how to formulate open-ended questions and closed-ended questions, to specify research population, and to create a focus group, among others. Crane's study on female fashion magazine readers (2000), my study on Japanese designers in Paris (2004), and Muggleton's study on youth subculture (2000) are examined as examples of survey methods in fashion/dress studies.

WHAT IS A SURVEY METHOD?

A survey is a research method in which subjects respond to a series of statements or questions in a questionnaire or an interview. The survey is well suited to studying what cannot be studied directly by observation or participant observation discussed in Chapter 3, "Ethnography." The survey involves asking questions about opinions, beliefs, or behaviors, and this method is most frequently used by sociologists, economists, and marketers, although their research goals may differ.

For example, if we want to investigate whether there is a gender difference in terms of where men and women are more likely to buy clothes, we can take a survey and find that out. If a theory suggests that a person's social class determines one's taste in clothing/fashion, survey data can be collected to determine whether this might be true.

There are many data collection and measurement processes that are called surveys. They basically have the following characteristics (Fowler 2002):

1. The purpose of the survey is to produce statistics, that is, quantitative or numerical description about some aspects of the study population.
2. The primary way of collecting information is by asking people questions, and their answers constitute the data to be analyzed.
3. Generally, information is collected about only a fraction of the population, that is, a sample, rather than from every member of the population.

A survey targets a population, such as single women with high income living in big cities. Sometimes every adult in the country is the survey population, but obviously, contacting a vast number of people is impossible so researchers usually study a sample, a much smaller number of subjects selected to represent the entire population, that is, people who are included in your research, so that they can give answers to your research questions (Fowler 2002; Rea and Parker 2005).

Survey results are eventually converted into quantitative data, which can be considered a separate area of expertise and can be handled by professional statisticians. This chapter does not go into the statistical manipulation of the survey data and is not about statistical methods. Therefore, those without a background in statistics should be able to follow everything covered in this chapter. By understanding the whole survey research process, a researcher can prepare basic reports that analyze simple trends, supervise survey data collection, or become a sophisticated user of the survey data collected by others, known as secondary data analysis, which is discussed in Chapter 7, "Other Methodologies."

Survey method is a very practical tool that can be used not only by researchers in academia and students but also by fashion industry professionals, such as marketers or merchandisers. For instance, consumer attitudes toward the latest styles in fashion, the reasons why they prefer some styles over others, or the extent of celebrities' impact on popular fashion can be measured and analyzed.

Both interviews and questionnaires have their own weaknesses and strengths. Some of the advantages of this method are that self-administered questionnaires are inexpensive and useful and may receive greater responses from subjects in personal interviews. But there are possibilities that questionnaires may not be returned, and personal interviews are costly in time and money (Rea and Parker 2005). Although not all surveys involve interviewing, it is common to hire an interviewer to ask questions and record answers. When interviewers are used, it is important to avoid having them influence the answers respondents give, and at the same time to maximize the accuracy with which questions are answered. The interviewer's role and the role of the interviewee, rapport, and accessing difficult/sensitive materials and issues need to be taken into consideration in addition to various skills and techniques necessary for effective interviewing.

SAMPLING

As discussed briefly in Chapter 2, "Research Process," before you begin your survey, you must specify your research population. You first select a population, the entire group of people to be studied. If a population is relatively small, all of its members can be approached and interviewed. If a population is very large, it would cost too much time and money to contact all of its members. In such a case, we need a sample, a relatively small number of people selected from a larger population. The sample must accurately represent the entire population from which it is drawn. Otherwise, the information obtained from the sample cannot be generated to the population. Failing to remember this may produce misleading conclusions.

If a sample is to be representative, all members of the population must have the same chance of being selected for the sample. Selection, in effect, must be random, which is why a representative sample is often called a random sample. A crude way to select a random sample is to throw the names of all members of a population into a hat, mix them up, and then pull out as many names as needed for a sample. This method may be too cumbersome to use if the population is very large. There are more sophisticated and convenient techniques for drawing random samples from large populations. The methods most commonly used are systematic sampling and stratified sampling. Systematic sampling is the process of drawing a random sample systematically rather than haphazardly. It involves using a system, such as selecting every tenth or hundredth person in the population. In contrast, stratified sampling is used when the population can be divided into various strata or categories, such as males and females. To draw a stratified sample, we have to know what percentage of the population falls into each of the categories used and then select a random sample in which each category is represented in exactly the same proportion as it is in the population. Thus it is the process of drawing a random sample in which various categories of people are represented in proportions equal to their presence in the population (Thompson 2002).

CASE STUDIES

Case study methods involve systematically gathering information about a particular person, social setting, event, or group to allow the researcher to effectively understand how the subject operates or functions (Feagin, Orum, and Sjoberg 2001). The case study is not actually a data-gathering technique but a methodological approach that incorporates a number of data-gathering measures. The approach of case studies ranges significantly from general field studies to the interview of a single individual or group. They may focus on an individual, a group, or an entire community and may also utilize a number of data-gathering technologies such as life histories, documents, oral histories, in-depth interviews, and participant observation.

The qualitative researcher uses the case study approach as a guide to his or her research. Rich, detailed, and in-depth information characterize the type of information gathered in a case study.

A case study is a many-sided investigation of a single social phenomenon, and it is usually seen as an instance of a broader phenomenon, as part of a larger set of parallel instances (Feagin, Orum, and Sjoberg 2001). It also allows the research to include the natural setting of the subject. Your case study might be a new emerging designer in London or a new Haute Couture house in Paris. You may also wish to study or analyze a series of case studies of related social phenomena.

By concentrating on a single phenomenon, individual, community, or institution, the research aims to uncover the manifest interaction of significant factors characteristic of this phenomenon, individual, community, or institution. But in addition, the researcher is able to capture various nuances, patterns, and more hidden elements that other research approaches might overlook. The case study method tends to focus on holistic description and explanation, and any phenomenon can be studied by these methods.

FOCUS GROUPS

Focus group refers to a research technique that explores group reaction to a particular topic. The members of a focus group need have no previous acquaintance with each other. It is defined as an interview style designed for small groups. Using this approach, researchers strive to learn through discussion about conscious, semiconscious, and unconscious psychological and sociocultural characteristics and processes among various groups. Focus group interviews are either guided or unguided discussions addressing a particular topic of interest or relevance to the group and the researcher (Edmunds 1999). A typical focus group consists of a small number of participants. The informal group discussion atmosphere of the focus group interview structure is intended to encourage subjects to speak freely and completely about behaviors, attitudes, and opinions that they may have.

You may sometimes wish to conduct a group interview, for example, an interview with several members of a youth subculture at one time. As one member of a group responds, other members may be reminded of similar experiences or they may wish to add details that they consider important.

For example, you want to investigate why some people are obsessed about or even worship one particular designer brand. Then you want to select a focus group who only wears specific brands. You will probably find a great deal of commonalities and similarities in their shopping behavior, beliefs, and attitudes toward a particular brand.

When focus groups are administered properly and successfully, they are extremely dynamic. Interactions among and between focus group members stimulate discussions in which one participant reacts to comments made by another. It is important to have a facilitator or a moderator who is experienced in interviewing focus groups. The moderator may use a single standard set of questions, asking each one in turn, which may lead into active discussions. In that way, you may be able to obtain difficult-to-gather information. This method has become an integral part of data-collection technology among qualitative researchers.

QUESTIONNAIRES

Survey questionnaires are widely used in social sciences, such as sociology and economics and also by diverse interest groups. The choice of language can influence the outcome of the questionnaire survey.

Beyond selecting subjects, the survey must have a specific plan for asking questions and recording answers. The most common way to do this is to give subjects a self-administered questionnaire with a series of written statements or questions. The researchers let subjects choose possible responses to each item, as in multiple-choice questions or closed-ended questions in which answers are either yes/no or one word/phrase. By creating a survey instrument, the social science researcher may not be creating new knowledge that will become part of ordinary usage. By requiring a respondent to answer the survey instrument with its limited choices, the respondent may have to select a choice that is not precisely his or her opinion. Your research question needs to be very clear prior to making a questionnaire. Each item/question in a questionnaire should relate to a specific objective of your research. Unless your items/questions are well crafted and formulated, you will not be able to achieve your research objectives (Thompson 2002).

A researcher may occasionally want subjects to respond freely, to permit all opinions to be included. In that case, open-ended questions are created. Many researchers prefer open-ended questionnaires. The researcher asks additional questions depending upon the subject's responses to an initial question. Such data are more difficult to organize and analyze but this technique is often a rich source of additional qualitative insight into the matter being studied.

Open-ended questions may be appropriate when exploring a topic that is new to the researcher. If there was no literature or very little literature on the topic, you can conduct a pilot study in which people are asked open-ended questions. Their responses in the pilot study[1] can be used as the basis for writing items with choices in the main study. When considering the use of open-ended questions, keep in mind that many respondents are often turned off if they think that they have to write a well-crafted essay. It becomes too much like a test and can even be time-consuming. You may want to ask them to jot down some ideas or points. If you need to ask many open-ended questions that require extensive responses, you should consider using face-to-face interviews instead of a questionnaire so that your respondents do not need to write anything.

WRITING ITEMS TO COLLECT DEMOGRAPHIC INFORMATION

Demographic items/questions are often included in questionnaires. These request information on background characteristics, such as sex, age, race, ethnicity, level of education, income, religion, and so on. Sometimes the information is needed in order to fulfill a research objective. These questions should be asked sparingly. You do not need to ask anything that is unrelated to your research objective. Asking a large number of demographic questions will make your questionnaire longer, and long questionnaires often get a lower response rate than short ones. Also, the more demographic questions you ask, the more likely it is that respondents may view the questionnaire as being intrusive into their privacy. Therefore, try to keep the demographic questions as short as possible. You may be able to reduce the need to collect demographic information by using information that is already available to you. For example, if you are distributing questionnaires only to high school seniors, most likely they are seventeen or eighteen years old so it is unnecessary to ask their age.

WRITING ITEMS TO MEASURE ATTITUDES

Questionnaires can be used to measure attitudes. An attitude is a general predisposition toward groups of people, organizations, and institutions, among others. When you measure attitudes, you ask questions about feelings, actions, and potential actions in the future (Fowler 2002). For example, we can measure people's attitude toward the latest trends, such boys wearing pink or other traditionally female colors. To measure this, we can write items that ask respondents how they feel about shopping pink clothes or what they think about their fathers, husbands, boyfriends, or male partners wearing pink. Is it appropriate or inappropriate? Is it socially acceptable or unacceptable?

In the 1930s, Rensis Likert[2] advocated the use of items that ask respondents to indicate the extent to which they agree or disagree with statements. This is an attitudinal scale. To write a Likert-type item, write a simple declarative statement and follow it with choices that ask for the respondents' level of agreement, such as strongly agree, agree, neutral, disagree, strongly disagree. Use "Don't know" in Likert-type items sparingly since you would rather avoid answers that provide no specific answers, and it does not give you any information to analyze.

PREPARING STATISTICAL TABLES AND FIGURES

The process of making questionnaires is qualitative, but the results of the questionnaires, that is, closed-ended questions, are converted into numbers and made into statistical data. Those data can be presented as tables and graphs so that an analysis can be made (answers to open-ended questions remain qualitative). If the questionnaire is not complex, you can probably do the calculations yourself. Assuming that the results are done by statisticians, you have the results in your hand, and you can create statistical tables and figures.

PREPARING A TABLE OF FREQUENCIES

If you are reporting separately on each questionnaire item, the first step in the analysis is to determine how many respondents marked each choice. The letter "f" for frequency of response or "N" or "n" is used.

Example

Age	Number of respondents	%
20–25	90	45
26–29	50	25
30–35	40	20
36 and above	20	10
	N = 200	100%

For attitude scales, you score each item and sum the scores on the items to get a total score for each respondent. The total score indicates the degree to which a respondent has a positive attitude toward the object of the scale. When analyzing the results using such a scale, the first step in the analysis is to determine how many respondents earned each total score and to organize the data into a table.

Calculate percentages and arrange them in a table with the frequencies: A percentage is calculated by dividing the part by the whole and multiplying by 100. A major advantage of percentages over frequencies is that they make the results comparable across two or more groups of unequal size. A common misconception among beginning researchers is that all groups of respondents must be equal in order to make legitimate comparisons of the groups.

Example

Q: How do salespeople in upscale department stores in New York treat you? (N = 200)

Rating	Excellent	Very Good	Fair	Poor	Very Poor
N	14	35	98	32	21
%	7	17.5	49	16	10.5

GRAPHS

For nominal data, consider constructing a bar graph. Nominal data are measures of identity, and this separates results into two or more distinctive features; nominal scales label or name individual or groups of things into categories (Flynn and Foster 2009). If you ask respondents to name, for example, their gender, religion, college major, these become nominal data. For example, values can be given to race/ethnicity, such as 1 = White, 2 = Hispanic, 3 = American Indian, 4 = Black, 5 = Asian, and 6 = Other. However, nominal data does not lend itself to being translated into a set of sequenced numerical scores, and the usual method of analysis for nominal data is to compute percentage. These may be presented in a table, bar graph (vertical or horizontal), or pie chart. Each table and figure should be given a number and a title called a caption. A polygon consists of connected dots if distributions of scores are to be compared. Dashed lines are used at both ends to make it look like it is resting on the base.

Examples
Vertical Bar Graph

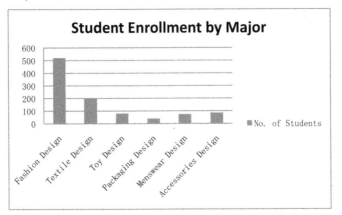

Pie Chart

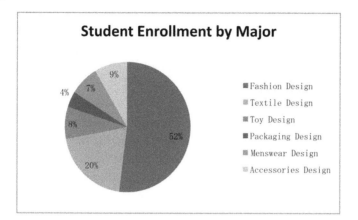

Polygon

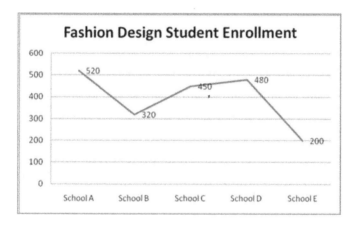

Which types of tables and figures you use to present a single set of scores is a matter of personal preference.[3] When presenting sets of scores for two or three groups, polygons are superior because they permit a drawing using different kinds of lines for each group on the same set of axes.

INTERVIEWS

Researchers must determine the nature of their investigation and the objectives of their research (Bordens and Abbott 2007). It provides a starting point and helps the researcher develop a schedule of questions for interviews. Unlike a questionnaire, an interviewee is not required to write anything. He or she simply responds to your questions.

In an interview, a researcher personally asks subjects a series of questions, thereby solving one problem common to the questionnaire method, that is, the failure of some subjects to return the questionnaire to the researcher. Another difference is that interviews give participants freedom to respond as they wish. Researchers often ask follow-up questions to clarify an answer or to probe a bit more deeply.

Interviewing may be defined as a conversation with the purpose of gathering specific information about a topic one is studying. While it may seem to be a very simple method, it is not as easy as one may think. The purpose should be clearly spelled out, and the questions need to be formulated in such a way that you get the information and answers you are looking for. Interviewing usually involves a face-to-face interaction. This type of interview is more formal rather than informal. It takes place in a structured setting rather than a natural setting. There are some differences between interviews as part of the survey and interviews in an ethnographical study.

TWO TYPES OF INTERVIEWS

The interview is an effective method of collecting information for certain types of research questions, and for addressing certain types of assumptions. There are two types of interviews, the choice depends on what the research topic is and how large the sample size is.

1. Structured Interviews

More formally structured

No deviations from question order

Wording of each question asked exactly as written

No adjusting of level of language

No clarifications or answering of questions about the interview

No additional questions may be added

Similar in format to a pencil-and-paper survey

Researchers using this technique have fairly solid ideas about the things they want to find out during the interview. They assume that the questions scheduled in their interview instrument are sufficiently comprehensive to elicit from subjects all information relevant to the study. All respondents are asked the same questions. Even if the subjects mention something that may interest you and be beneficial to your research, you cannot alter the questions you have provided them. The first step in increasing interviewer consistency is to give them standardized questions. Interviewers need to be trained in how to administer a survey so as to avoid introducing important biases in the answers obtained.

2. Semi-structured Interviews

More or less structured
Questions may be reordered during the interview
Wording of questions flexible
Level of language may be adjusted
Interviewer may answer questions and make clarifications
Interviewer may add or delete questions for each interviewee

In semi-structured interviews, some questions are fixed while others are not fixed and may be followed up with additional questions. In an unstructured interview, open-ended questions are asked and respondents are allowed to answer freely, in their own words, and there are hardly any questions that are prepared beforehand.

MUGGLETON'S INTERVIEW STUDY ON YOUTH SUBCULTURE

Muggleton clearly explains his research strategies in his study on fashion subcultures. He gives fieldwork details and interview schedule as an appendix at the end of his book. He interviewed a total of fifty-seven different people (forty-three male and fourteen female), in thirty-eight separate interviews. The age range was sixteen to thirty-four; the average age was twenty-four (Muggleton 2000: 171). All but three interviews (involving six subcultural informants) were conducted in Brighton, East Sussex, in six separate visits: September 1993, December 1993–January 1994, April 1994, July–September 1994, January 1995, and April 1995 (2000: 171). Muggleton explains the process as follows:

> The interview can best be described as semi-structured, often conversational, and the order of the questions was not always strictly adhered to. Informants would sometimes initiate the discussion and provide a more promising line of inquiry to be followed, or they might pre-empt my intended order of questioning. Nor was the wording of the questions particularly important, for I treated them as areas for discussion. After each fieldwork session the questions were slightly revised to take account of new themes and hypotheses generated inductively from the data.... All interviews were taped and transcribed. The duration of the interviews varied considerably, from twenty minutes to one and a half hours, with the typical time taken being around forty minutes. (Muggleton 2000: 171–2)

Interview Schedule from Muggleton's Study

- How old are you?
- What job (or otherwise) do you now do?
- What different jobs, if any, have you done previously?
- What jobs do (did) your parents do?
- Do you think of yourself as identifying with a particular sort of people because of the way you dress?
- How long have you been dressing like this?
- What made you choose the way you look, your style?
- What were the main influences for you? Where did you get your ideas about the style from?
- Where do you get your various items of clothing from?
- Do people who dress in this way tend to have anything in common apart from the style? (particular way of life, attitudes or ideas, way of behaving, music?)
- What's the difference between people who dress like you and people who dress more conventionally?
- Do you ever feel ties or bonds with other (whatever) people who you see dressed in a similar style, even if you don't know them personally?
- What are your views on people who dress "straight" or conventionally?
- In what ways do you think you are similar to or different from conventionally dressed people? (Muggleton 2000: 172–3)

In addition to interviews, Muggleton selected several subcultural informants for the study on the basis of what he regarded as their unconventional appearance.[4]

CRANE'S FOCUS GROUP STUDY ON FASHION MAGAZINE READERS

Crane introduces feminist and postmodern feminist views on fashion. Fashion has been viewed as hegemonic by encouraging women to be dissatisfied with their appearance and to make regular changes in their clothing in order to conform to changing definitions of style. Crane uses women's responses in focus groups to representations of gender in fashion photographs and clothing advertisements to explore whether their perceptions of themselves correspond to the ways women are represented in these images (2000: 204). Before conducting her study, she raises a number of research questions as follows:

1. Do these women see themselves as being able to project identities offered by the fashion press, or do they seek clothing that corresponds to their own conception of their identities?

2. How do they interpret complex visual messages that represent a highly conflicted dominant culture in which female identity is subject to continual negotiations?

The goal of her study is to examine responses to representations of gender in fashion photographs and clothing advertisements among young and middle-aged women, representing diverse ethnicities and nationalities. Photographs that exemplify different aspects of hegemony as it has been conceptualized in fashion magazines were selected in the study:

a. Hegemonic femininity: sexuality/pornography
b. Hegemonic poses as interpreted by Goffman (1979): ritualization of subordination and licensed withdrawal
c. Violations of traditional norms of feminine demeanor (traditional hegemonic femininity): frontal gaze and eye contact, nudity and androgyny and gender ambiguity, as well as subjects who conformed to these norms

Eighteen of these photographs were chosen from the February, March, and September 1997 issues of *Vogue,* of which a subset of six to nine photographs was shown to members of each focus group. The photographs included fashion editorial photos and clothing advertisements.

First, before showing members of focus groups any of these photographs, they were asked to complete a short questionnaire that indicates their background, their level of interest in fashion, and the ways they follow fashion. They were asked several questions designed to elicit their perceptions of these photographs and the extent to which they were able to identify with the models in the photographs. They were assured that all answers will be kept entirely confidential, and no one will be identified by name in any publication based on this research.

- How frequently do you read *Vogue*?
  - ___ Every month
  - ___ Several issues a year
  - ___ Occasionally
  - ___ Never
- Do you read any other fashion magazines regularly (at least several issues a year)?
  - ___ Yes ___ No
  - If Yes: Which ones?
- Do you attempt to keep up with current fashion?
  - ___ Yes ___ No
  - If Yes: In what sense? (Please check as many as apply)
  - ___ Specific styles of the season
  - ___ Specific accessories (shoes, bags, belts)
  - ___ Clothing items displaying brand names

- • ___ Adjusting hemlines
- • ___ Other. Please explain.
- • If No: Why not?
- ■ How do you find out about fashion? (Please check as many as apply)
  - • ___ "Cool" friends, relatives
  - • ___ Television
  - • ___ Fashion magazines
  - • ___ What pop singers are wearing
  - • ___ What people are wearing on the street
  - • ___ What's in my favorite store. Please give name.
  - • ___ Catalogues: Which ones?
  - • ___ Other. Please explain.
- ■ What are you wearing right now?
- ■ What is your favorite outfit at the moment?
- ■ What color clothing do you usually wear?
- ■ What is your major?
- ■ What year are you in?
- ■ What career do you hope to pursue after college?
- ■ What is your father's occupation?
- ■ What is your mother's occupation?
- ■ Where are you from? _____ (city) _____ (state)
- ■ Where did you grow up? _____ (city) _____ (state)
- ■ What is your race? (Crane 2000: 256–7)

Their responses were analyzed according to the following questions: Did these women accept the "authority" of fashion as exemplified by the fashion press? How did they respond to the different social agendas that were represented in the photographs? Did age, race, and ethnicity affect women's responses to the photographs? Were participants able to detect the presence of gender and racial stereotypes?[5]

The next step was the focus-group interview. During the interview, they were asked to respond to clothing advertisements and editorial photos taken from recent issues of *Vogue* magazine. Participants in the focus groups were shown a series of six to nine photographs. The following questions were asked about each photograph:

- ■ What aspects of this photograph do you like?
- ■ What aspects of this photograph do you not like?
- ■ What adjectives would you use to describe the image of the woman (women) in this photograph?
- ■ Whose point of view is this photograph intended to represent?
  - • ___ A man's point of view
  - • ___ A woman's point of view

- Does it represent your point of view?
- Whose point of view does this photograph actually represent?
  - ___ The fashion editor's point of view
  - ___ The fashion designer's point of view
  - ___ The advertising account executive's point of view
  - ___ The photographer's point of view
- Would you like to look like this woman (women) on certain occasions? Why? Or Why not?
- What meanings does the clothing in the photograph convey?
  - ___ Masculinity
  - ___ Femininity
  - ___ Androgyny
  - ___ Sexuality
  - ___ Professionalism
  - ___ Other
- Would the clothes in the photograph influence in some way how you dress? If Yes: How? If No: Why not? (Crane 2000: 255)

KAWAMURA'S STUDY ON THREE CASE STUDIES OF JAPANESE DESIGNERS IN PARIS

My study on Japanese designers in the French fashion system applies a case study approach (2004). Three types of Japanese designers in Paris were selected. These typologies are:

Type 1: Kenzo who assimilated into French culture completely

Type 2: The Japanese Avant-Garde Designers who introduced an unconventional, definitely non-Western look

Type 3: Hanae Mori who is the only Asian and Japanese couturière in the exclusive Haute Couture organization

In investigating the entry process of a foreign designer into the world of French fashion, we must pick designers who already belong there. Non-Western designers are particularly more interesting as research subjects because they have less resources and social connections. After establishing the three types, I go further to locate other Japanese designers in Paris and see how each one connects to each other and also how they are connected to these three types indicated in the beginning.

As indicated earlier in this chapter, case studies represent other cases, or they illustrate some particular trait, characteristic, or problem. They provide insights into an issue or refine a theoretical explanation. They are investigated in-depth and all aspects and activities are detailed but not simply to elaborate the case per se. Instead the intention is to assist the researcher to better understand some external theoretical question or problem. They may or may not be viewed as typical of other cases. Using case studies, researchers explore in-depth a program, an event, an activity, a process, or one or more individuals. The cases are bounded by time and activity, and researchers collect detailed information using a variety of data-collection procedures over a sustained period of time.

Furthermore, case studies of organizations may be defined as the systematic gathering of enough information about a particular organization to allow the researcher insight into the life of that organization. This type of study might be fairly general in its scope, offering approximately equal weight to every aspect of the organization. For instance, I conduct an organizational case study on the fashion trade organization in Paris. Subgroups and divisions, such as Haute Couture and Prêt-à-Porter, within the organization are examined. The results provide a thorough understanding about how the organization operates and how each subdivision within the organization fits together and serves the overall objectives and functions of the organization. There are other fashion trade organizations in the world, but I select the one in Paris as a case study since it is the oldest one.

There are a number of reasons that a particular organization may be selected for a case study. For example, a researcher may undertake a case study of an organization to illustrate the way certain administrative systems operate in certain types of organizations. Or the researcher may be interested in accessing how decisions are made in certain types of organizations or even how communication networks operate. The case method is an extremely useful technique for researching relationships, behaviors, attitudes, motivations, and stressors in organizational settings.

I also conduct a community case study of fashion, Japanese fashion designers in Paris in particular. A community can be defined as some geographically delineated unit within a larger society. Such a community is small enough to permit considerable cultural or subcultural homogeneity, diffuse interactions and relationships between members, and to produce a social identification by its members. Case studies of communities can be defined as the systematic gathering of enough information about a particular social group to provide the researcher with an understanding and awareness of what things go on in that community; why and how these things occur; who among the community members take part in these activities and behavior; and what social forces may bind together members of this community. You could focus on a community in general, or you may want to focus on some particular aspect or phenomenon of the community. Within the world of fashion that I call the fashion system, there are different communities, that is, different occupational groups and roles that individuals play. By studying the fashion community, I see how the fashion institutions and industries are connected to the trade organization and also investigate individuals within each community and how those individuals are linked to one another.

The following semi-structured interview questions were asked of designers and nondesigners who are directly and indirectly related to the fashion trade organization in Paris:

■ What is the purpose of the organization?
■ What role does the organization play in the French fashion industry?
■ What are the organizational functions?
■ Why do you think the organization lasted for more than a century?
■ What was the purpose of creating the subdivision, the Chambre Syndicale du Prêt-à-Porter des Couturières et des Créateurs?
■ Is Haute Couture a realistic business?
■ What are the difficulties in maintaining the couture houses and the organization itself?
■ Will the organization last despite the financial crisis of couture houses?
■ Who elects the members of the organization?
■ Is it more difficult for foreign couturières to become members?
■ What are the advantages of being a member of the organization? (Kawamura 2004: 173)

The following semi-structured interview questions were asked of Japanese fashion designers in Paris:

■ How did you get started in France?
■ Why are you (partially) based in Paris?
■ Why do you need to show your collections in Paris? Would you have the courage not to show your collections in Paris?
■ Would you be able to maintain your current reputation without showing your collections in Paris?
■ Would you have been this famous had you not come to France?
■ Being a foreigner, have you ever had any difficulties penetrating into the French fashion system?
■ What were the steps you took to be elected as a member of the Chambre Syndicale?
■ Were you looking for Western acceptance of Japanese style?
■ How important is it for you to belong to the French fashion system or American fashion system? Why not just stay in the Japanese system? (Kawamura 2004: 173–4)[6]

CONCLUSION

There are data that can only be gathered through administering questionnaires and conducting formal or informal interviews. We must understand how to plan questionnaire research and how to write questionnaire items, assemble and administer them, analyze them, and write up reports and findings. Researchers also must be aware of choosing the right research population and a representative of that population. The results that are generated quantitatively can be represented as figures and graphs.

GUIDE TO FURTHER READING

Bordens, Kenneth, and Bruce Barrington Abbott (2007), *Research Design and Methods: A Process Approach,* New York: McGraw-Hill.

Crane, Diana (2000), *Fashion and Its Social Agendas: Class, Gender, and Identity in Clothing,* Chicago: University of Chicago Press.

Edmunds, Holly (1999), *Focus Group Research Handbook,* New York: McGraw-Hill.

Feagin, Joe R., Anthony M. Orum, and Gideon Sjoberg (eds.) (2001), *The Case for the Case Study,* Chapel Hill: University of North Carolina Press.

Fowler, Floyd J. (2002), *Survey Research Methods* (3rd edn), Applied Social Research Methods Series, Vol. 1, Thousand Oaks, CA: Sage Publications.

Kawamura, Yuniya (2004), *The Japanese Revolution in Paris Fashion,* Oxford, UK: Berg.

Muggleton, David (2000), *Inside Subculture: The Postmodern Meaning of Style,* Oxford, UK: Berg.

Rea, Louis M., and Richard A. Parker (2005), *Designing and Conducting Survey Research: A Comprehensive Guide,* Hoboken, NJ: Jossey-Bass.

Thompson, Steven K. (2002), *Sampling,* Hoboken, NJ: Wiley-Interscience.

5 SEMIOTICS/SEMIOLOGY

Objectives

- ■ To trace the development of semiotics/semiology.
- ■ To explore Ferdinand de Saussure's semiology and later development.
- ■ To understand Roland Barthes's contribution to fashion/dress studies.
- ■ To learn Lehmann's semiotic study of Alfred Hitchcock's movie.
- ■ To examine Lurie's study on analogy between language and clothes.
- ■ To recognize Barnard's interpretation of semiotic analysis of fashion/dress.
- ■ To describe the relationship between semiology and poststructuralism.

Many scholars shy away from semiotics or semiology[1] because of Roland Barthes's complex application of semiotics to fashion in his famous book *The Fashion System* (1990). In this chapter, I first explain how the discipline of semiology started, developed, and spread and introduce some contemporary studies on fashion/dress that use a semiotic analysis in their empirical research.

Semiotics, or semiology, is the science of signs and is any system of signification. Semiotics derives from the linguistic theory of Ferdinand de Saussure (1857–1913), a Swiss linguist, who stresses that signs are arbitrary and derive their meanings only from oppositions to other arbitrary signs used in a system. His approach was extended by the French literary theorist Roland Barthes, who argues that any item of culture, including clothing and fashion, can become signs and communicate meanings. Semiotics is used in fashion/dress studies as an analytical tool in treating fashion/dress as a text and in decoding the meaning of every clothing item. It does not have to be tangible clothes but written texts.

There are scholars who apply a semiotic analysis to fashion and dress. In order for us to understand it, we need to trace the development of the discipline and refer to Saussure who is known as the father of semiology. Barthes's work on fashion/dress, which emerged primarily out of Saussure's work, is explored so that we understand how material objects, such as clothing items, create meanings, and how these meanings are reproduced. Lehmann (2000), Lurie [2000 (1981)], and Barnard (1996) refer to a semiotic study in less complex ways to discuss fashion and dress. Semiotics are also used to decode and analyze fashion advertisements and photographs.

SAUSSURE'S THEORY OF SIGNS

We must understand Saussure's theory of signs before we begin to talk about a semiotic analysis of clothing and fashion made by various scholars. Saussure is an early twentieth-century linguist. Before Saussure, linguistics concentrated on the way languages have developed, the search for the common ancestor, the emergence of modern languages, the pronunciation of words, and the etymology of words, among other things. However, Saussure had a very different perspective. Influenced by Emile Durkheim, a French sociologist, he pointed out that language is not an individual but a collective representation.

Language as a formal system is a set of relationships among different words and parts of speech. It has a force imposed by society, and there are correct and incorrect ways of speaking, which are not determined by the individual. The language as a system has a structure with its own rules, such as the order of words in a sentence, grammar, and how words are uttered, among other things. The underlying structure imposed by society should be the topic of linguistic analysis, according to Saussure (1966 [1916]).

Geertz argued that his analysis of the concept of culture is a semiotic one and the whole semiotic approach to culture is to aid researchers in gaining access to the conceptual world in which our subjects live so that we can converse with them (Geertz 1973: 24), and he insisted that the analysis of culture is not an experimental science in search of law but an interpretive one in search of meaning (Geertz 1973: 5). This is in opposition to Saussure's attempt to make semiotics an autonomous science (Saussure 1966 [1916]). Saussure proposed semiology, the general science of signs, although it remained just an idea until the 1960s. Then other scholars such as anthropologists and literary critics sought to profit from its methodological insights and found themselves developing the semiological science that Saussure had postulated at the turn of the century.

LANGUE VERSUS *PAROLE*

Saussure made an important distinction between *langue* and *parole*. *Langue* is the linguistic system, that is, what one learns when one learns a language, and *parole* is speech that consists of the countless spoken and written utterances of a language, that is, an organized structure of signs whose meaning depended on their differences from one another. Semiology attempts to describe the underlying system of rules and distinctions that makes possible signifying events. Semiology is based on the premise that insofar as human actions and objects have meaning, there must be a system of distinctions and conventions that generate the meaning consciously or unconsciously. Saussure's achievement lies in his systematic elaboration of a general science of signs, and that is called a semiology. Saussure emphasizes that the signs are essentially arbitrary, and therefore, it enables signs to be combined in so many ways to convey so many different meanings since they are flexible.

THE TWO LEVELS OF THE SIGN SYSTEM

Furthermore, according to Saussure, there are two levels to the sign, the signifier and the signified, and both of them together create the sign. But the relationship between the signifier and the signified is arbitrary, according to Saussure (1966 [1916]).

The signifier can be a word, a sound, or an image, but in case of fashion/dress studies, we often apply the sign system to objects and images. The signified is not a real tangible object but it is something that the signifier refers to. The signified can vary between individuals or context while the signifier is more stable. The signified is the concept, the meaning of the thing indicated by the signifier. The signifier without the signified has no meaning whatsoever, and it simply exists. The signified cannot exist without the signifier either. Therefore, the sign needs two levels. Our social life is filled with the signs that have these two levels.

BARTHES'S CONTRIBUTION TO FASHION/ DRESS STUDIES

Barthes, following Saussure and other modern linguists, maintains that what is interesting about language is how the structure works, and he applies Saussure's semiology[2] to mundane objects of everyday life, such as wrestling, wine, or film, and argues that these objects could become signs and communicate meanings. Fashion can convey a message about the social status or the occupation of its owner or about their worldviews and beliefs, among other things. So can any item of culture, ranging from styles of dress or food to popular entertainment. Like Saussure, he also explains the arbitrary nature of the signs.

For example, Barthes explains that food can be studied as a sign system as well. There is the food system of culture, that is, *parole,* that consists of all the events of eating while *langue* is the system of rules underlying these events. These rules determine what is edible, which dish goes with what or contrasts with other dishes, and each dish is combined to form a course meal. A restaurant menu represents a sample of a society's food grammar in which there are conventions to the ordering of items, start-ing with a soup or an appetizer, then a main dish, and lastly a dessert. If the dessert comes before the soup, that would be against the conventions and also considered ungrammatical in linguistic terms. Similarly, the contrasts between dishes within a class, such as the main course and the dessert, bear meaning. Therefore, the task of a semiologist like Barthes is to reconstruct the system of distinctions and conventions that enable a group of phenomena to have the meaning they do for members of a culture.

Barthes's *Mythologies* (1972) is a compilation of a series of articles he wrote monthly in a magazine called *Les Lettres Nouvelles* between 1953 and 1956, and it is one of his most influential writings. He discovered that various linguistic terms could give insight to a new perspective on cultural phenomena, and he embraced the possibility of studying all human activity as a series of languages. Saussure's ideas of the signi-fiers and the signifieds display the ideological contents of various activities. Barthes discussed different aspects of mass culture, and he made an attempt to analyze the so-cial stereotypes that often are passed off as natural and taken-for-granted things that no one ever questions. His attempt was "to track down, in the decorative display of what-goes-without-saying, the ideological abuse which, in my view, is hidden there" (1972: 11).

What does he mean by "myth"? Myth for Barthes means a delusion to be exposed. There is always the second order, which is the mythical meaning that Barthes wants to investigate and expose. Any objects and practices, even the most utilitarian, function in the same way and are endowed with second-order meaning by social usage. He is concerned with the image of fashion and dress. His focus is not the raw materials of garments or how they are made. He explores the second-order meanings attached to it by social convention. Beginning with myth as delusion, Barthes then later empha-sizes that myth is a form of communication, a "language," a system of second-order meaning. Myth is a product of the interplay between direct and indirect meanings. *Mythologies* was a study of how meaning and value occur and are created in everyday life. The signs of everyday life were the mark of ideology and cultural formation, according to Barthes (1972). Language is not a natural phenomenon but is a set of conventional signs.

In *The Fashion System* (1990), Barthes conducted a large, semiological study on fashion/dress. Instead of giving an account of the clothes advertised in the French publications *Le Jardin des Modes, Elle, l'Echo de la Mode,* and *Vogue* during a six-month period in the late 1950s, he concentrated exclusively on the language used by the editors and fashion writers. Language is a system of signs, and a sign unites an image that may be the sound of a spoken word or the way it is written. Fashion is a system that creates meaning by having different shapes and silhouettes of garments with various details and by connecting different pieces of garments together. But he is not looking at the actual clothes but at the descriptions about the clothes. Barthes (1990: 10) writes: "[I]t's meaning that sells clothes." To describe this system, Barthes reads captions on the assumption that the captions represent the aspects of the clothes that make them fashionable and thus enable him to identify the distinctions at work in their sign system. Barthes insisted that it is not the objects that are the subject of analysis but rather the discourse or text that are about the objects. He explains that clothes are not themselves immediately signs but rather, they become subject to the signs of the world of fashion; that is to say that the cultural world of talking and writing about clothes gives the clothes themselves a social meaning (Barthes 1990). How the clothes are described/written in words determines whether they are going to be treated as fashion or not.

LEHMANN'S SEMIOTIC STUDY ON ALFRED HITCHCOCK'S MOVIE

Lehmann (2000) makes a semiotic analysis of a movie by Alfred Hitchcock. His methodological approach is the combination of cinema and semiotics and analyzes an espionage thriller film called *North by Northwest* directed by Hitchcock for release in July 1959. He argues that the film and the role played by Cary Grant are explained best by looking at appearances. Lehmann selects the dozen scenes in which the suit explicitly works as a signifier on screen or is topical for the dialog, thus carrying a significance that considerably exceeds its function within the storyline (2000: 468).

He insists (2000: 468): "The sartorial details observed in the following are not to be taken as metaphors for behavioral patterns, nor are they meant to be symbolic for the character's psyche. They should be read first as visual signifiers within a semiotic analysis." He explains that the suit as the sartorial surface functions as a signifier in an old-fashioned narrative that tells of the hero's trials and tribulations, and it shows him being pursued, ridiculed, and assaulted until he liberates himself from normative constraints to gain first freedom of action, and then love and respect as an individual (2000: 469–70). He reviews scene by scene explaining the characters in the movie wearing suits and makes a semiotic analysis of the visual interpretations of the suits as follows in one of the scenes in the movie:

> In the ensuing struggle, Thornhill is forced on the sofa and plied with Bourbon; the suit is seriously assaulted and soiled for the first time. Indeed, here one begins to read "suit" exclusively as a signifier and the character as the signified: the hero is defined through his surface and the suit in the course of the film's narrative concentrates on the garment, whose light gray wool absurdly

distinguishes the fugitive in his quest....The fact that the cloth and shape of the suit show remarkable endurance and make a complete recovery from the pursuits and assaults in the preceding scenes, must be read as Hitchcock's effort to present the hero as a stable and identifiable commodity to the audience. (Lehmann 2000: 472–3)

The suit is the parole, using Saussure's and Barthes's term, and it has a visual cinematic narrative. A simple object such as a male suit speaks volumes.

LURIE'S STUDY ON ANALOGY BETWEEN LANGUAGE AND CLOTHES

According to Rose (2005), one of the most commonly applied models for linking the interpretation of modern clothing and texts is semiotics, drawn from linguistics theory. As explained earlier, this theory relies on a separation between the meaning of "signified" and its physical embodiment, the "signifier." However, the problem of semiotic analysis has been summarized by Miller as "subordinating the object qualities of things to their world-like qualities" (1987: 95) and also "ignoring the ways that textiles create meaning through their embodiment of financial, aesthetic and haptic values" (Miller 1987: 95). Miller instead sees objects as "type-tokens...both an individual form and an example of a larger category to which it must be related" (1987: 127).

Lurie is well known for her study that makes a direct analogy between language and clothes (2000 [1981]) and rejects the idea of its arbitrary relationship. She argues that language is just like clothes, and clothes just like language. We use language to communicate verbally, and we also use clothes to communicate nonverbally. The more vocabulary you know, the more sophisticated your speech will be. In the same manner, the more clothes you have, the more sophisticate and stylish you will look. She explains clothing as a sign system[3] as follows:

> [I]f clothing is a language, it must have a vocabulary and a grammar like other languages...as with human speech, there is not a single language of dress, but many (like Dutch and German) closely related and others (like Basque) almost unique. And within every language of clothes there are many different dialects and accents, some almost unintelligible to members of the mainstream culture. Moreover, as with speech, each individual has his own stock of words and employs personal variations of tone and meaning. (Lurie 2000 [1981]: 4)

The vocabulary of dress includes not only items of clothing, but also hair styles, accessories, jewelry, make-up, and body decoration (2000 [1981]: 4). Lurie makes an analogy with a sharecropper, and argues that the language of a sharecropper, for instance, may be limited to five or ten "words" from which it is possible to create only a few "sentences" almost bare of decoration and expressing only the most basic concepts. A so-called fashion leader, on the other hand, may have several hundred "words" at his or her disposal, and thus be able to form thousands of different "sentences" that express a wide range of meanings (Lurie 2000 [1981]: 4–5). Unlike Saussure or Barthes, for Lurie, the signs are not arbitrary. There is no skepticism between language and clothes, both of which are used as texts.

BARNARD'S FOCUS ON SEMIOTICS IN SOCIAL INTERACTION

Semiotics or semiology is known as esoteric and complex, but some fashion/dress scholars dissect it to a level that is understandable to students. As Saussure explained, the fundamental idea in semiology is that there are the two levels, the signifier and the signified, which are two separate concepts.

Barnard explains (1996: 29) that the reading of semiotics occurs within social interactions, and we are communicating via signs and symbols that constitute the two levels mentioned above. However, unlike the language, the structured system of meanings is not that fixed, absolute, or definite. As Saussure and Barthes insist, they are arbitrary. Barnard explains: "[C]ommunication makes an individual into a member of a community; communication as 'social interaction through messages' constitutes an individual as a member of a group" (1996: 29).

Barnard further explores the sender and the received of the sign and says that:

> The semiotic model also seems more plausible on the matter of how meanings are generated. . . . It is no longer the case that either the designer or the wearer or the spectator of the garment is the source of the intentions that provide the meanings; on the semiotic model, meanings are the result of negotiation between these roles. (Barnard 1996: 30–1)

Meanings are constantly produced, exchanged, negotiated, renegotiated, and reproduced, and the meanings of the original garment are given numerous interpretations by numerous cultural producers and the garment ends up with a set of meanings different from those with which it began (Barnard 1996: 31). Thus Barnard's semiotic interpretation of clothes is the polar opposite of Lurie's.

Like Barnard (1996), Eco also looks at social life as a sign system and writes:

> I am speaking through my clothes. If I am wearing a Mao suit, if I were without a tie, the ideological connotations of my speech would be changed. Obviously fashion codes are less articulate, more subject to historical fluctuations

than linguistic codes are. But a code is no less a code for the fact that it is weaker than other stronger ones. Gentlemen button their jackets, shirts, and coats from left to right, ladies from right to left. Suppose I were speaking of semiotics, standing in front of you, buttoned from right to left: it would be very difficult for you to eliminate a subtle connotation of effeminacy, in spite of my beard. (Eco 2007: 144)

Such arbitrariness leads scholars to believe fashion/dress is ambivalent in nature since the signs are ambivalent. We need to explore further to what extent a semiotic analysis of fashion and clothes gives accurate meanings of these objects.

CONDUCTING SEMIOTIC ANALYSIS OF VISUAL MATERIALS

Williamson (1978) is one of the pioneers who conducted a semiotic analysis of advertisements in magazines. Advertisements give added values to commercial products by making them meaningful to potential consumers. The fashion industry where visual materials are crucial can make a good use of this methodological strategy.

Stokes gives clear step-by-step explanations of a semiotic analysis of texts:

Select object of your analysis: If you are studying fashion magazines, your research subject included in your research question or hypothesis must correspond to the target readers of the magazine you select. If your research population is fashionable women in their 40s, do not choose *Teen Vogue* as an analytical tool.

Collect texts/visual materials for your analysis: How many or how much materials you need to collect depends on the depth of your research and on your research question. But if you are conducting a social scientific study, it is desirable to look at several visual materials and not just one so that you begin to see similarities and commonalities from the data you gather.

Explain and analyze the materials: Examine the materials carefully and explain everything you see in the image, such as objects, colors, people's poses and their outfits among many other elements. Then you can begin to decode the meaning of each item in the image treating them as a sign. You can see the relationship between the visual image and the linguistic signs. Furthermore, explain the cultural knowledge and background and experience required to understand the implications of the image.

Make generalizations and draw conclusions: As the decoded implications become a code, you can see whether this code is found in other materials. If it is found, it means that you are able to make generalizations about the meanings of the code and can even bring out a theory. In conclusion, you must explain if your analysis and interpretation support or negate your hypothesis. (Stokes 2003: 73–5)

SEMIOTICS AND POSTSTRUCTURALISM

Structuralism that appeared in the latter half of the twentieth century is one of the most popular approaches in investigating culture, society, and language. Both Saussure and Barthes are known as structuralists who study a specific area as a complex system of interrelated parts.

Barthes, who was an advocate of Saussure and structuralism, moves on from Saussure's views, and this is why he is often referred to as a poststructuralist since he went beyond Saussure's theory of signs. While Saussure explained that the relationship between the signifier and the signified is arbitrary, Barthes now says that it is better to describe this relationship as not arbitrary but "motivated," which implies that the relationship is not a natural one but is still inseparable from "arbitrary." Placing linguistic or nonlinguistic signs in their social contexts explains how and why they work (Barthes 1972).

In this way Barthes's thinking links him with other poststructuralists, especially Jacques Derrida (1930–2004), a French philosopher known as the father of postmodernism and deconstructionism. Barthes also suggests "the death of the author," which creates the freedom of the reader. In this respect, he recognizes that there is no final authority for deciding the meaning of a text, just as there is no final meaning attached to a sign because it is constantly changing according to its context. Therefore, poststructuralism is known as the theoretical formulation of postmodern conditions that reject boundaries between different categories.

CONCLUSION

Saussure was the first to suggest an idea and a new discipline called semiology, a study of signs that have no actual content. There is no natural connection between the signifier and the signified that make up the sign, but once established, that very system or configuration of signs exists as a distinctive entity that can be studied within a specific context. The Saussurean model is founded on a premise of the linguistic sign's arbitrary nature that bears directly on the development of Barthes's own semiology. Contemporary scholars in fashion/dress studies also adopt the method to investigate the second-order or the signified of an object, such as clothes, or to understand how clothes become fashion through written texts.

GUIDE TO FURTHER READING

Allen, Graham (2003), *Roland Barthes,* London: Routledge.

Barnard, Malcolm (1996), *Fashion as Communication,* London: Routledge.

Barthes, Roland (1972), *Mythologies,* trans. Annette Lavers, New York: Farrar, Straus and Giroux.

Barthes, Roland (1977), *Elements of Semiology,* trans. Annette Lavers and Colin Smith, New York: Hill and Wang.

Barthes, Roland (1990), *The Fashion System,* trans. Matthew Ward and Richard Howard, Berkeley: University of California Press.

Barthes, Roland (2006), *The Language of Fashion,* Oxford, UK: Berg.

Berger, Arthur Asa (1998), *Signs in Contemporary Culture: An Introduction to Semiotics,* Salem, WI: Sheffield Publishing.

Eco, Umberto (2007), "Social Life as a Sign System," in Malcolm Barnard (ed.), *Fashion Theory: A Reader,* pp. 143–7, London: Routlege.

Lehmann, Ulrich (2000), "Language of the PurSuit: Cary Grant's Clothes in Alfred Hitchcock's 'North by Northwest,'" in Christopher Breward (ed.), Masculinities: Special Issue, *Fashion Theory: The Journal of Dress, Body and Culture,* 4/4: 476–85, Oxford, UK: Berg.

Lurie, Alison (2000 [1981]), *The Language of Clothes,* New York: An Owl Book/Henry Holt.

Saussure, Ferdinand de (1966 [1916]), *Course in General Linguistics,* translator unknown, New York: McGraw-Hill.

Stokes, Jane C. (2003), *How to Do Media and Cultural Studies,* London: Sage Publications.

Thibaul, Paul J. (1997), *Re-reading Saussure: The Dynamics of Signs in Social Life,* London and New York: Routledge.

Williamson, Judith (1978), *Decoding Advertisements: Ideology and Meaning in Advertising,* London: Boyars.

6 OBJECT-BASED RESEARCH

Objectives

- To learn what object-based research is, who the method is used by, and how it is used.
- To examine the historical development of object-based research and understand why it was devalued.
- To explore the connection between object-based research and material culture studies.
- To explore some specific studies using the object-based research method.
- To understand the importance of making object-based research interdisciplinary by incorporating other methods, such as oral history and archival materials.

In Chapters 3 to 5, methodologies in qualitative research, such as ethnography and interviews, were examined. This chapter discusses an object-based research method often used by costume historians, museum curators, and art historians rather than by sociologists, psychologists, or cultural anthropologists, since their focus is the object or the artifact itself, such as dress and clothing. As far as the method of inquiry in fashion/dress studies is concerned, it is no surprise that those who closely study dress as a tangible object adopt object-based research since fashion is represented through dress and clothing, which is a tangible, material object. But we must also point out that the object itself does not speak about its symbolic social or cultural meanings, so it requires other methodologies unless you are analyzing the physical features of the clothing, such as fabric texture, sewing techniques, or the silhouette of the dress. Today, fashion/dress scholars combine this method with other methods and take an interdisciplinary approach in their research. In this chapter, I discuss the development of the object-based research method and explore how it was used and by whom. Studies that combine other methodologies, such as oral history and archival records, are also examined.

WHAT IS OBJECT-BASED RESEARCH?

As Wilson (1985: 48) explains, traditionally, the study of fashion and/or clothing has been a brand of art history and has followed its methods of attention to detail, and comparable to the study of furniture, painting and ceramics, a major part of its project has been accurate dating of costume, assignment in some cases of "authorship," and an understanding of the actual process of the making of the garment, all of which are valid activities. Historians and art historians (Boucher 1987 [1967]; Breward 1995; Cunningham 2003; Davenport 1952; Hollander 1993, 1994, 2000, 2001; Koda and Martin 1993, 1995a,b, 1996; Palmer 2001; Steele 1985, 1988, 1991; Tortora and Eubank 2009; Welters and Cunningham 2005) look at clothing and dress items over extended periods, and they explain repeated regularities and fluctuations and decode the cultural meanings of dress and clothing.

Museum curators and costume historians also conduct object-based research in the museum's historical costume collections, and the objects are the primary source of information. They explore the history of the artifacts and of the contexts within which they have meanings. We can learn about the object in relation to other objects, peoples, ideas, and specific historical time periods. It allows the researcher to look directly at objects and investigate their colors, shapes, silhouettes, construction, and sewing techniques involved, and describe the observations of their physical characteristics. The examination of the objects can lead to other social, cultural, historical, political, artistic, or technological research questions.

Object-based research examines minute details and channels through a series of acquired skills and interpretative methods. You first need to find the clothing object, then identify it, conserve it, display it, and interpret it. This method can be incorporated into a variety of theoretical interpretations, but it has the basic theory in common, and that is the exploration of material culture in relation to immaterial culture, which is explained later in this chapter. The danger of object-centered methodologies is that they may be restricted by too close a focus on aesthetic or physical considerations.

THE HISTORICAL DEVELOPMENT OF OBJECT-BASED RESEARCH

Just as a social hierarchy among social classes and individuals exists, there was and still is a hierarchy among different disciplines; some disciplines have a higher status with more prestige than others in academia, and thus they have more research funding opportunities. There is also a hierarchy among different research methodologies. When the method is mostly adopted by female researchers, the method itself begins to lose its value, and object-based approaches were often taken by female historians such as Elizabeth McClellan, Betty Kirke, Doris Langley Moore, and Anne Buck. The feminization of fashion that made fashion a female affair with the Industrial Revolution had lowered the value of fashion practice itself, but the method also followed a similar trend in its devaluation.

Therefore, it was mostly women who collected and curated collections of Euro-American fashionable dress, and Taylor explains the subordinate position that clothing artifacts were placed in:

> Though women anthropologists have argued convincingly that serious analytical research of the manufacture and function of ethnographical garments was granted only a lowly place in the hierarchical ranking of research interests until the last quarter of the twentieth century, dress was always equally included in anthropology collecting and display policy. The same cannot be said for museums of Western European decorative arts. (Taylor 2004: 67)

Working in a male-dominant occupation, curators treated fashionable European dress as marginal cultural objects that were never considered valuable. Therefore, there was a masculine bias in the museum collections, such as the robes of the orders of chivalry and the uniforms. Nothing that alluded to female or femininity was included in the collections. There was nothing objective about the selection of museum objects. Its function as a central cultural force was quite simply neither understood nor accepted (Taylor 2004: 105). However, Taylor explains a gradual shift in their views:

> A fundamental shift in Britain away from these male-oriented approaches to analyzing fashion was set in place from the late 1940s through the work of two women curators: Doris Langley and Anne Buck. Building on the work of Talbot Hughes and Thalassa Cruso, they both made major contributions from 1949. These have in many ways proved more influential than those of C. W. Cunnington and James Laver, perhaps because, as curators, both worked from the closest object-based analysis. Neither shared the Laver/Cunnington view that the world of women's fashions centred on attracting the opposite sex. (Taylor 2004: 58–9)

There was an explosion of costume/dress–related publications between 1931 and the late 1960s that gave many scholars the opportunity to study dress from a historical perspective, and they continued to use the object-based method.

Therefore, a collection of fashionable dress worn by wealthy women in Europe did not exist in the museum collections for a long time since they were considered insignificant and of no value; at the same time, the object-centered research was often dismissed or completely neglected, and the study of dress in general was marginalized or looked down upon in academia as nonacademic. Taylor writes that the history of the development of museum collections of dress has remained a neglected research field (2004). Then at the turn of the century, new theories of fashion were proposed by scholars, such as Thornstein Veblen and Georg Simmel:

> Methodologies were radically altered between 1899 and 1904 when sociologists Thornstein Veblen and Georg Simmel turned their attentions to assessing the role of Western dress within patterns of class behaviour and gendered consumption. This opened up serious theoretical approaches to analysis of the form and function of fashionable dress though response from within the field of dress history was extremely slow. (Taylor 2004: 44)

However, many museum curators and costume historians continued to follow the traditional approach, that is, object-centered studies.

VARIOUS STUDIES USING OBJECT-BASED RESEARCH

Instead of taking readers step-by-step through this research methodology, it is probably easier to understand if I introduce various studies using the object-based method.

McClellan's work on the history of American costume 1607–1800 (1969) uses a different approach to dress studies that was still new at the time. In her book, McClellan studies clothing worn in Spanish, French, English, Dutch, Swedish, and German settlements in early North America. She was a female researcher, and she worked from a strongly object-based approach. She borrowed clothing directly from their owners and used photographs and drawing of surviving garments. She focused on everyday working-class clothes, which no other scholar had done before 1906.

Arnold (1977), a textile and dress historian, explored dress history through meticulous analysis of the cut and patterns of English male and female dress, using the surviving garments. As Arnold writes:

> [O]bjects act as reminders and confirmers of our identities, and probably our idea of our identity relies more in such objects than it does in any idea of ourselves as individuals [then collections] have the capacity to take on a male and female identity: collecting, collectors, and collectible objects are all potentially gendered...through the gender associations of the objects collected; and through the gendered use of collections. (Arnold quoted in Pearce 1992: 55)

The interdisciplinary, object-based approach was one that was very familiar to Arnold, and her research was predicated on a detailed understanding of dress gained by the close examination of surviving garments, and she recorded this process with sketches, photographs, and copious notes.

Palmer (1997: 299) explains that recent important scholarly development and esca-
lating interest in costume from other disciplines demonstrate that it is imperative for
traditional fashion historians to apply a more critical, theoretical, and analytical methodology in their research. She studies couture dresses worn in Toronto in the postwar
years and develops multidisciplinary methodology (1997). For example, she studies a
Schiaparelli evening dress very closely that was donated by a wealthy lady in Toronto,
reads its label, and examines the numbers of alternations on the dress, which is all based
on the material object. She then conducts documentary and archival research and lo-
cates the design sketch in Paris and also finds photographs of the lady in the same Schiaparelli dress published a few times in different publications (Palmer 1997: 304–5).

OBJECT-BASED RESEARCH AND MATERIAL CULTURE STUDIES

Instead of leaving object-based research on its own, many scholars must transcend
the investigation of the objects and put it in a larger perspective within the context
of material culture studies in order to avoid being narrow in research focus. Barnard
succinctly explains the problem of object-based research as follows:

> The most significant problem is that the notion of "identification" or factual
> description presupposed that it is possible to give an "objective" account of
> the "object itself" without the influence of any cultural preconceptions. Any
> words that one uses to describe the object will exist and be meaningful within
> a language, and that language will inevitably contain and communicate any
> number of cultural preconceptions. (Barnard 2007a: 8)

Thus, material objects, such as clothing and dress, can be placed in the material culture studies that demands not only an object-based approach but also a combination
of different methods. As Taylor (1998) suggests, those who research clothing and
dress need to go beyond the traditional form of object-based research.

Scholars from various disciplines, such as anthropology, sociology, cultural studies, photographic studies, and media studies, all share common interests in material
culture, practices of representation, the interpretation of cultural texts, and com-
prehending social relations and individual experience, and each area of study has its
particular theoretical and methodological heritage. Material culture studies shows us
that we all live within, act through, and are shaped by the material world. There is no
human being who is not surrounded by material goods. Culture and material goods
are inseparable, and thus they must be studied simultaneously.

However, Miller (2005) explains a conflict between two perspectives to material
culture studies. There are two factions: (1) those trained in textile conservations, design

or museum collections, experts in the analysis of cloth and textiles, and (2) social scientists in cultural studies, sociology, or social anthropology with training in semiotic and symbolic analysis and an interest in the "social life" of clothing. Miller explains:

> Specialists in textiles may have very little respect for those disciplines they lump together as "cultural studies." They see this social analysis as merely mapping differences in clothing and fashion onto social categories such as class, ethnicity and gender.... In turn, social scientists may denigrate scholars of textile, pattern, form and technology as "positivists" who study such things merely because they have collections. (2005: 1)

Material culture studies should incorporate multiple perspectives and must transcend them so that as Miller proposes, there must be the integration and reintegration of materiality with sociality because there is no simple boundary or distinction between persons and their social environment. Eicher was one of the fashion/dress scholars who emphasized the social context of material objects. Clothing and dress are one of the most important and richest aspects of material cultures. Once viewed simply as mere artifacts, cloth and clothing are now recognized as culturally constructed commodities with complex symbolic properties, transmitting purity and pollution, linking past and present, transforming through belief, carrying fundamental values (O'Connor 2005: 41). Kroeber (1919) and Kroeber and Richardson (1940) were the first to study Western dress in a detailed and systematic manner exploring the relationship between social and political influences on clothing-fashion.

MAKING OBJECT-BASED RESEARCH INTERDISCIPLINARY

Like Miller, Javis (1998) also discusses a split between object-based researchers and fashion/dress scholars who do not adopt such methods. Javis explains:

> There is a current divergence between object-based study, carried out by museum curators and makers of reproduction dress, and university studies of dress and fashion, usually based on written sources, images and statistics, but rarely on the real thing... the gulf between academics and curators has not been fully closed but bridges have been built, and communication prospers. (Javis 1998: 300)

We need to explore the ways in which a more inclusive or interdisciplinary approach in fashion/dress studies can be taken so that we can examine the relationship between fashion and textiles from a material culture perspective to question traditional methods of display and established discourses in fashion and textile history.

Many scholars enhance their archival and object-based research by considering additional sources and employing innovative approaches to the material objects at hand. There is a growing interest in fashion and dress by various disciplines. Kramer (2005: xi) writes: "because of the prevalence of textiles and dress in every aspect of human life, a multiplicity of disciplines has taken notice of these objects, including art and design history, history, media and cultural studies, gender studies, material culture studies, studies in consumption, museology, sociology, and anthropology, to name a few." While dress or textiles themselves are a key source, they cannot be read and analyzed in isolation, and they need to be situated in a contextual model built up from all the available different sources. This is how the researchers begin to tell a story about the objects.

OBJECT-BASED RESEARCH AND ORAL HISTORY

Oral history accounts are recognized as important sources for the study of textiles and dress (Biddle-Perry 2005; Burman 1999; Eastop 2005; Lomas 2000). It is essential to employ an interdisciplinary methodology, including design history, fashion and textiles history and theory, oral history and discourses arising from anthropology and cultural theory. Turney writes:

> Interdisciplinarity was intended to widen the sphere of reference, bridging gaps of knowledge marginalised or trivialised by single methodologies.... The emphasis on first-hand experience, particularly in relation to tactile and emotive objects such as clothing, adds an extra dimension to the study of fashion and textiles that goes beyond designer intent and notions of the avant-garde. (Turney 2005: 59)

Meanings and interpretations based on subjective information, such as oral history, are not without problems since self-reports and their validity may put into question, but oral history as a method can be used to investigate dress and textiles produced by cultures that are not predominantly text-based.

BREWARD, CONEKIN, AND COX'S STUDY ON EVERYDAY CLOTHES IN THE UNITED KINGDOM 1940–1980

Breward, Conekin, and Cox (2002b) explain the significance of an individual's surviving collection of female everyday clothing and other related items that were donated to the London College of Fashion by Mrs. Cecile Korner's sons. Following a period of cataloguing and some initial research, a selection of items was displayed in simultaneous exhibitions at the college and at Judith Clark Costume Gallerie in London's Notting Hills. The authors write (2002a: 2): "[T]he content of the collection, though not of museum standard, nevertheless allows us a privileged glimpse at the fashionable choices of one woman whose tastes and needs were informed by her social context and period. Indeed, it was the seeming 'ordinariness' of the archive which...made it so attractive as a teaching and research collection." These clothes believed to have been bought between the late 1940s and the 1980s give an extraordinary insight into "conservative" middle-class mores during the postwar years (Breward, Conekin, and Cox 2002a: 1). This object-based study is enhanced by the method of oral history. A son recalls his mother's style and appearance:

> [M]y mother always dressed for dinner, I mean she always dressed for my father when he came back from the office. In the morning she would get up and wear a white blouse, dark blue skirt, flat shoes and usually a dark blue cardigan and that was her uniform until lunch time, and that was how she did the housework and got the day going....At lunch time she would change into a day dress if she went out to lunch or whatever, and then in the evening she would wear something very simple like...black velvet. (2002a: 3–4)

People's narratives are the evidence of a person's past history and life. They shed light on who Mrs. Korner was, what she was like, and the kind of lifestyle she had when she was alive. Such data can only be collected through oral history as well as object-based research.

TURNEY'S STUDY ON FLORAL FLOCKS IN THE UNITED KINGDOM

Turney's (2005) paper focuses on oral testimony and the ways in which responses to artifacts offer the potential for reappraising established notions of what it is to be fashionable, as well as highlighting the disparities inherent in the dissemination of styles, motifs, techniques, and fabrics. Furthermore, she wanted to investigate the experience of what it might be like to actually wear these garments (Turney 2005: 58). She writes:

> Clothing is what people wear, and derives from "cloth" or fabric that is suitable for wearing. Fashion, however, is culturally constructed and refers to process and changes in styles—it is dynamic, about change, movement and aesthetics....With this in mind, the experience of wearing specific items of

clothing is central to the formation of an understanding of the self within the wider world, yet this more subjective appraisal of fashion is rarely evidenced in exhibitions. (Turney 2005: 58)

Turney's investigation draws from oral history testimonies that have been central to collaborative research projects between Bath Spa University and the Museum of Costume Bath, which aimed to address the significance of the floral printed dress in the twentieth century, culminating in an exhibition called "Pick of the Bunch," a Web site, and publication. Turney explains the significance of oral history as a method in her research:

> Oral testimony regarding the consumption of such garments, including purchase and the actual experience of wearing, became a fundamental aspect of uncovering why certain garments were deemed fashionable, or were valorized outside of a traditional design history methodology. (2005: 59)

Turney's oral history respondents were selected from replies to an advertisement placed in the local daily newspaper called *The Bath Chronicle*. The Bath respondents were all more than fifty years old and offered a valuable insight into growing up in the 1950s and 1960s. But it was necessary to look for younger respondents with whom to compare experiences and to demonstrate if concepts of fashionability and floral dresses differed in terms of time and location, so a group of ladies between the ages of twenty-five and thirty-five years old, working in professional occupations in London, formed a contrasting focus group. It is important to note that these were merely sample groups, and responses may well have differed should other groups have been sought or the sample widened. Therefore, the potential for interpretation and reinterpretation of responses to floral printed dresses can be varied. Different groups can provide alternative fashion histories.

A lady who is quoted in Turney's study remembers shopping with her mother in the 1950s: "I would shop with my mother in department stores in London. She was a fashionable woman who had impeccable taste. She always chose my clothes, which were watered-down versions of her own; not quite so grown up, girlish and floral." Turney explains:

> Oral history enabled an assessment and appreciation of garments outside of design and fashion history methodologies. Personal recollection about what was worn by whom and when, as well as evocative experiences of the actual wearing of garments informed the selection of objects for display. In this respect, oral history proved to be a tool which allowed visitors to the exhibition with no prior knowledge of fashion and its histories to engage with the display on a personal level. (Turney 2005: 63)

OBJECT-BASED RESEARCH AND WRITTEN ARCHIVAL DOCUMENTS/LITERARY SOURCES

While fashion/dress studies rarely relies solely on written documents/literary sources, it can be combined with object-based research. There are many object-centered historians and curators working in museums who use dress and textiles as a primary source of evidence. They integrate evidence from material objects and written documents to investigate historical practices, such as trade and consumption, in depth.

Handley (2005) compares textiles discovered in the archaeological excavation on Egypt's Red Sea Coast from the Roman (between the first and the third centuries) and Islamic (between the eleventh and the fourteenth centuries) periods, rare material culture, with documentary sources. She refers to written regional documents, such as the first-century merchant's guide that helps the interpretation of the textiles. Documents can provide more information than a straightforward list of items that can be "checked off" against archaeological finds (Handley 2005: 10). Textual/written records can help archaeological interpretation to understand how the textiles were used and understood in the past.

Furthermore, Rose (2005) focuses her research on the sale and consumption of women's quilted petticoats, which were universally worn and widely sold as one of the first ready-to-wear garments traded throughout Britain. She refers to the literature on eighteenth-century consumption, texts, and textiles. People use wills, invoices, probate inventories, and other textual sources. Trade cards, commercial documents, can also be the subject of the study.

Mikhaila and Malcolm-Davies (2005) study the dress of ordinary Tudor men in the sixteenth century. The research offers insights into the wardrobes of ordinary Elizabethan men based on the Essex wills left by laborers, sailors, servants, and the lower-status craftsmen and tradesmen, such as carpenters, blacksmiths, bakers, and butchers. The Essex Record Office has published a series of volumes compiled and edited by F. G. Emmison between 1983 and 2000. "Each of the ten published volumes of Essex wills was examined for references to clothing and textiles. These were categorized by garment or accessory type and by color and fabric where specified by the testator" (Mikhaila and Malcolm-Davies 2005: 18). This study systematically examined a vast number of documents, enabling conclusions to be drawn on the conventional use of certain garments, fabrics, and colors by Tudor men of relatively modest means.

CONCLUSION

Object-based research used by historians, art/costume historians, and museum curators has gone through a transition, and there has been an attempt among the dress/fashion scholars in general to put it within the context of material culture studies so that a split between object-based research and the research focused on social and cultural symbols and meanings can be filled. Many object-based researchers combine the method with other methodological strategies while taking interdisciplinary approaches by incorporating other methods, such as oral narratives and archival materials.

GUIDE TO FURTHER READING

Arnold, Janet (1977), *Pattern of Fashion: Englishwomen's Dresses and Their Construction,* London: Drama Publishing.

Hayward, Maria, and Elizabeth Kramer (eds.) (2005), *Textiles and Text: Re-establishing the Links between Archival and Object-based Research,* London: Archetype Publications.

Mikhaila, Ninya, and Jane Malcolm-Davies (2005), "What Essex Man Wore: An Investigation into Elizabethan Dress Recorded in Wills 1558–1603," in Maria Hayward and Elizabeth Kramer (eds.), *Textiles and Text: Re-establishing the Links between Archival and Object-based Research,* pp. 18–22, London: Archetype Publications.

Miller, Daniel (2005), "Introduction," in Susanne Kuchler and Daniel Miller (eds.), *Clothing as Material Culture,* pp. 1–19, Oxford, UK: Berg.

Palmer, Alexandra (1997), "New Directions: Fashion History Studies and Research in North America and England," in Valerie Steele (ed.), *Fashion Theory: The Journal of Dress, Body and Culture,* 1/3: 297–312, Oxford, UK: Berg.

Summers, Leigh (2001), *Bound to Please: A History of the Victorian Corset,* Oxford, UK: Berg.

Taylor, Lou (2004), *Establishing Dress History,* Manchester, UK: Manchester University Press.

Turney, Jo (2005, July 26–28), "(Ad)Dressing the Century: Fashionability and Floral Frocks," in Maria Hayward and Elizabeth Kramer (eds.), *Textiles and Text: Re-establishing the Links between Archival and Object-based Research,* AHRC Research Centre for Textile Conservation and Textile Studies, Third Annual Conference, pp. 58–64, London: Archetype Publications.

Wilson, Elizabeth (1985), *Adorned in Dreams: Fashion and Modernity,* Berkeley: University of California Press.

7 OTHER METHODOLOGIES

Objectives

- To learn other qualitative research methodologies, such as oral history, secondary analysis, ethnomethodology, and cross-national research, among others.
- To understand the integration of quantitative and qualitative methods.
- To explore different fashion/dress–related studies that use methodologies not discussed in previous chapters.
- To identify how different methodologies can be mixed in one research.

So far in this book, I have discussed some of the major qualitative research methods often used by scholars in fashion/dress studies, but they are by no means exhaustive. When we study fashion, there is a wide range of sources that we use, such as written documents, visual materials, and objects/artifacts (Whitaker 2007). In this chapter, I briefly explore some other methodological tools that can be used or may be used in the research. Ideally, any research, not just fashion or dress, should adopt multiple methods so that information can be collected from different sources to get more accurate and convincing findings. It is the job of a researcher to come up with the best and the most appropriate methodologies in acquiring the best possible answers to the research questions. By combining and applying different methodologies, fashion/dress studies can include interdisciplinary perspectives. Other possible qualitative methodologies in fashion/dress studies, such as archival records, historiography, and ethnomethodology, among others, are examined, some of which have already been discussed in Chapter 6, "Object-based Research."

Qualitative research is multimethod in focus, often involving an interpretive, naturalistic approach to its subject matter (Trumbull 2005). It means that qualitative researchers study things in their natural settings, attempting to make sense of, or interpret, the phenomena in terms of the meanings people bring to them. Qualitative research involves a variety of empirical materials, such as case study, personal experiences, life story, interview, observational, historical, interactional and visual texts, that describes routine and problematic moments and meanings in individual's lives. The qualitative approach is inductive with the purpose of describing multiple realities, developing deep understanding and capturing everyday life and human perspectives. It is a process of discovery of the phenomena being studied; consequently, it tends to be guided by broad research questions based upon some theoretical framework.

ARCHIVAL RECORDS AND HISTORICAL RESEARCH

Archival records are documents rather than artifacts or published materials, although collections of archival records may include artifacts and books. Archival records may be in any format, including text on paper or in electronic formats, photographs, motion pictures, videos, sound recordings. Unlike ethnography or interviews, this is an unobtrusive research strategy. Archival material is virtually nonreactive to the presence of the researcher. All the unobtrusive strategies amount to examining and assessing human traces. What people do, how they behave and structure their daily lives, and even how humans are affected by certain ideological viewpoints can all be observed in traces people either intentionally or unintentionally leave behind.

Archival records can be divided into public archival records and private archival records. If they are public, records are viewed as prepared for the expressed purpose of examination by others. Public records are written in more or less standardized form and arranged in the archive systematically, for instance, alphabetically, chronologically, and numerically indexed and catalogued. The term "archive" brings to mind some form of library, but any records that are registered are archive. On the other hand, personal documents involve any written record created by the subject that concerned his or her experiences. The common types of documents classified under this label include autobiographies, diaries/journals, letters and memos written by a subject in a research investigation. Photographic and video records may also serve as categories of personal documents.

For instance, in Ko's study of Chinese women's foot-binding practices, she acquires written sources from travel accounts and general descriptions of China published in Europe and the United States from the sixteenth to the early twentieth centuries (1997). Ko found these sources held in original form in the James Duncan and Stephen Phillips Libraries of the Peabody Essex Museum in Salem, Massachusetts (1997: 5). In her study of the Italian Fascists' unsuccessful attempt to control the fashion industry, Paulicelli (2004) analyzes various narratives in 1930s women's magazines, fiction, films, and also reviews the propagandistic objectives of Cesare Meano's *1939 Commentary and Italian Fashion Dictionary*, in addition to interviews with Italian designers.

Horwood (2002) explores the developments in the design of women's tennis wear in England during the interwar years starting with the pre–World War I norms, then in the 1920s, and then in the 1930s. She provides us with a specific example of English clothing as it was understood in the interwar years. She collects newspaper articles and other printed sources, such as *Lawn Tennis Bits and Pieces* (1930), *Diary of a Provincial Lady* (1934), and *Modern Tennis* (1933), and examines images of dress, gender, and modesty associated with the "quintessential English sport of tennis."

While it is uncommon in social sciences or material culture studies, depending on the focus of the research, the researcher may focus solely on written texts as evidence without referring to any other source. Rocamora (2001) investigates newspaper reports on high fashion shows of the British newspaper *The Guardian* and the French newspaper *Le Monde* during the year 1996. She argues that in both newspapers a field of fashion is constructed that is articulated around different beliefs: the belief in fashion as popular culture in *The Guardian* and the belief in fashion as high culture in *Le Monde*. She reviews all the articles, essays, and commentaries written about fashion shows in Paris and London. In this case, visual materials are simply treated as supplementary sources.

Historiography or historical research is an examination of elements from history. The term "history" is used synonymously with the word "past" and in turn, refers conceptually to past events of long ago. From a social science perspective, history is an account of some past event or a series of events. Historiography in fashion/dress studies is a method for discovering from records and accounts what people wore and what happened during some past period, and it involves far more than the mere retelling of facts from the past. It is more than linking together tired old pieces of information found in diaries, letters, or other documents, important as such an activity might be. Historical research is at once descriptive, factual, and fluid. It has nothing to do with one's nostalgic or sentimental feelings. It is social scientific research that values objectivity. Thus, it attempts to systematically recapture the complex nuances, the people, meanings, events, and even ideas of the past that have influenced and shaped the present.

The sources of data used by historiographers are the same as those of many other social scientists, such as confidential reports, public records, government documents, newspapers editorials and stories, essays, songs, poetry, folklore, films, photographs, artifacts, and even interviews or questionnaires. They classify these various data into primary sources or secondary sources. Primary sources involve the oral or written testimony of eyewitnesses. They are original artifacts, documents, and items related to the direct outcome of an event or an experience. They may include documents, photographs, recordings, diaries, journals, life histories, drawings, mementos, or other relics. On the other hand, secondary sources include the oral or written testimony of people not immediately present at the time of a given event. They are documents written or objects created by others that relate to a specific research question or area of research interest. These elements represent secondhand accounts. Secondary sources may include textbooks, encyclopedias, oral histories of individuals or a group, journal articles, newspaper stories, and even obituary notices.

ORAL HISTORY/ORAL NARRATIVE

Oral history or oral narrative can be used by historians, sociologists, or cultural anthropologists. As indicated earlier in Chapter 6, "Object-based Research," you can refer to oral or written testimony of individuals or interview individuals who are still alive and ask them to reflect back and remember their past experiences that are relevant to the research questions. Those narratives are valuable since the people had actually lived through that experience or events.

A documentary video called *The Theatre de la Mode* (1991) shows the revival of the French Haute Couture industry after World War II when France was liberated from the German Nazis. In the video, Robert Ricci, a son of famous French couturière Nina Ricci, talks about the social and economic situations and workers' labor conditions of the French fashion industry at the time. Also another lady who used to wear Haute Couture talks about her love for French fashion and remembers that she changed dresses a couple of times a day. Narrative research is a form of inquiry in which the researcher studies the lives of individuals and asks one or more individuals to provide stories about their lives (Clandinin and Connelly 2000). This information is then restored and retold by the researcher into a narrative chronology. In the end, the narrative combines views from the participant's life with those of the researcher's life in a collaborative narrative.

WRITTEN DOCUMENTS/LITERARY SOURCES

Although it is difficult to rely solely on written documents, historical or contemporary, they could be used as a supplementary material in the studies of fashion and dress. Since artists and designers may deviate from exact, visual representations, the accuracy of their pictures needs to be determined by other available data. One way to check is to refer to written descriptions and commentaries on dress of the same period in history, such as personal diaries, accounts of travel and exploration, catalogues, biographies, novels, memoirs, essays, satires, books of history and philosophy, and manuals on etiquette and personal conduct (Taylor 2002a). Religious writings can also be rich sources of information on dress, although they may be written for other purposes and have nothing to do with fashion per se. These written forms of evidence can provide information to help validate the authenticity of visual representations and to elucidate the meanings of dress within its contemporary setting, although they too may be subject to bias (Roach-Higgins and Eicher 1973: 15).

Scholars in literary studies use fiction and nonfiction as their sources, and some of them make an analysis of characters' outward appearance and how they are dressed through the written documents. While using the literary materials as a method is rare for social scientists, it is a viable qualitative method. These materials may be rich in costume descriptions and put the costumes in a particular social and cultural context. Buck (1983: 89) explains: "Where dress is used to express character and illuminate social attitudes and relationships, the novel can give more. It then shows dress in action within the novelist's world."

Some fashion/dress historians and researchers rely on novels, poetry, plays, newspapers, journals, autobiographies, and diaries as descriptive evidence. But the accuracy needs to be called into question. These materials need to be used with surviving garments.

Spooner (2004: 1) explains that both Gothic literature and the history and theory of fashion have achieved increasing prominence within academic discourse in the beginning of the twenty-first century. Costumes and disguises, veils and masks are ubiquitous features of Gothic fiction. She writes:

> According to Eve Kosofsky Sedgwick's seminal critical text, *The Coherence of Gothic Convention*s (1980, revised 1986), Gothic is fundamentally stagy and theatrical in its nature. From the giant helmet that falls on Walpole's Conrad in *The Castle of Otranto* (1764) to the costumes worn for contemporary Vampire Balls, clothing has always played a vital role in the construction of Gothic narratives. Indeed, the Gothic novel is historically linked to fashion through the emergence of modern consumerism in the eighteenth century. (Spooner 2004: 1)

ETHNOMETHODOLOGY

Ethnomethodology is the method people use on a daily basis to accomplish their everyday lives. It was founded by UCLA Professor of Sociology Harold Garfinkel in the 1940s. In his *Studies in Ethnomethodology* (1967), Garfinkel explained that so-called social order is internalized by actors who then act out those socially prescribed norms and values as Parson did, and how order is produced as the local achievement of those same actors.

Garfinkel coined the term "ethnomethodology" to refer to the study of folk (*ethno*) methods for making sense of the social environment. Ethnomethodologists draw a parallel between the methods that people use to reach an understanding of events, and the methods used by scientists. For them, the crucial problem in understanding social conduct is not simply about the values, ideas, perceptions that are expressed through behavior, but rather determining how they are assembled, communicated, manipulated, and used in social interaction.

Ethnomethodology is a study of how people convince themselves and one another that there is a stable order in society and of the nature of that order during and as a basis for social interaction. While some researchers dismiss the method as a nonscientific method and even trivial, it can be used in fashion/dress studies in challenging or testing supposedly stable dress codes. We have common ideas about how a dress should be made, how different items of clothing should look, how to wear them, and when to wear them. I have not come across any fashion/ dress studies that employ this methodology, but it can result in many convincing findings; for instance, wearing a dirty pair of torn jeans to a wedding, or a man wearing a pink sweater in public. You would find out that they are against society's dress codes through other people's responses and reactions. These are the things that many of us take for granted because these ideas are so deeply embedded in our minds.

SECONDARY ANALYSIS

The term "secondary analysis" is most often used in connection with survey data. Secondary analysis is defined as any further analysis of an existing dataset that presents interpretations, conclusions, or knowledge additional to, or different from, those presented in the first report on the inquiry as a whole and its main results (Hakim 1982: 1). Sometimes, it is not necessary to gather new information because of the availability of data collected previously by someone else. Sometimes, it is simply impossible to conduct an interview, observation, or experiment because the people we want to study are no longer alive. Thus, researchers often turn to analysis of existing data, which may be in the form of secondary analysis or content analysis.

In secondary analysis, which is an unobtrusive method, the researcher searches for new knowledge in the data collected earlier by another researcher; the original researcher had gathered the data for a specific purpose and the secondary analyst uses them for other purposes with their own unique research questions (Kiecolt and Nathan 1985). The data for secondary analysis are usually quantitative, presented in the form of numbers, percentages, and other statistics. But some of the existing information can be qualitative, in the form of words or ideas. Such information can be found in virtually all kinds of human communication, such as books, magazines, newspapers, movies, speeches, and letters, among others. To study human behavior from these materials, researchers often do content analysis, searching for specific words or ideas and then turning them into numbers. Analysis of existing data saves much time and money since the researcher is not collecting data but using existing data.

CROSS-NATIONAL RESEARCH

This method allows us to make comparisons between different countries on a particular topic. Researchers can look for similarities and differences to see why something happens in some countries while it does not happen in others. For instance, in some countries, a particular trend is popular while in other countries, it may not be so.

I study the French fashion system and explain how the system was established historically and how it is maintained. I examine the individual as well as institutional networks within the system and argue that fashion in France is highly institutionalized (Kawamura 2004). On the other hand, Rantisi (2006: 115–18) conducts a similar study and explores the institutionalization process of New York fashion. However, one of the biggest difficulties in comparing societies is the lack of comparable data, and thus, it is not easy to make cross-cultural comparisons. What sources, evidence, and data the researchers use varies widely.

Fashion's World Cities (2006), edited by Breward and Gilbert, has articles written about fashion cities around the world, such as Tokyo, Dakar, and Mumbai in addition to the major fashion cities, New York, Paris, Milan, and London, but each author focused on one city. It would not be an easy task for one researcher to cover a few cities and compare and contrast their industry structure or consumer preferences. Thus, a collaborative effort would be much encouraged in future fashion/dress studies so that the research perspective becomes not only interdisciplinary but even more global.

VISUAL AND AUDIO MATERIALS

Different types of visual records have been used to research dress and fashion. As part of visual culture, fashion is frequently being studied through illustrations, engravings, paintings, and photographs. Fashion/art/costume historians (Hollander 1993; Steele 1985) use historical visual materials, such as paintings, fashion plates, engravings, store catalogues, advertisements, and pamphlets, among others, as evidence to investigate how people dressed at a particular time period in history. Roach-Higgins and Eicher explain various methods that were used historically to record the way people dressed:

> Sculpture, paintings and ceramics…provided visual representations from very ancient times. Pictorial textiles and printed plates showing dress, as well as actual costume artifacts, are available from about the sixteenth century.…Costume histories summarize data from many of these sources. Modern costume histories are made more exact through the use of photographs of actual objects, often in color.…While contemporary items of dress are

readily available, artifacts are limited, and many are destroyed and have deteriorated. Costume plates and fashion plates were also used. (Roach-Higgins and Eicher 1973: 11–17)

Mackrell (2005) studies the close relationship between the paintings of Pisanello, who worked for several courts in Italy, and the clothes in his paintings during the Renaissance. His paintings depict the sartorial life of the Italian Renaissance courts. They were not simply paintings but were creating costume models and designing textile patterns and embroidery. Clark (1999) uses contemporary photographs, advertisements, calendar posters, and fashion magazines as evidence to show the development of the *cheongsam,* the Chinese ethnic dress, and how it represented modernity in the 1920s and 1930s.

Fashion scholars who study contemporary fashion/dress also use a great deal of visual and audio materials, such as photographs, illustrations, movies, and videos. Chen's study examines the sociopolitical meanings of official uniformity and differences and focuses on idealized dress as presented by the Chinese Communist Party (CCP) from 1949 to 1966 in sources such as photographs, posters, and film costumes (Chen 2005: 145), in addition to written sources, such as newspaper articles. Davis (1992) uses photographs and images to describe contemporary fashion while arguing people utilize fashion as a way to express their identity, and since their identities are ambivalent, so is fashion.

Some use recorded video or audio material produced for general and mass consumption. This may include television programs, transcripts, video tapes, DVDs and movies, among others. Baddeley (2002) referred to a number of Goth-related movies in his study. For those who study the relationship between fashion and photography (Antick 2002; Beard 2002; Cheddie 2002; Jopling 2002), visual materials are the indispensable, key sources of evidence in their study.

TRIANGULATION

One method is never sufficient to provide enough information on a subject one is studying. Harvey says that multidisciplinary approaches and methods allow one to appreciate dress as "the complication of social life made visible" (Harvey 1995: 17). Most researchers have at least one methodological technique they feel most comfortable with, which often becomes their favorite or only approach to research. This might be why many previous qualitative research texts often tend to lean toward a single research method, such as participant observation, interviewing, or one of the unobtrusive measures. Furthermore, they perceive their method as a nontheoretical tool, and they fail to recognize that different methods impose certain perspectives on reality. When researchers begin their research, a theoretical assumption has already been made.

Some researchers have combined the two research methods, quantitative and qualitative. For instance, narrative descriptions and statistics can be used since narrative data are able to support numerical data, and vice versa. This process is called triangulation. Each method reveals slightly different facts of the same symbolic reality. Thus, by introducing or using different methods, you obtain a better, more substantive picture of reality, a richer and more complete array of symbols and concepts.

The term "triangulation" is common in surveying activities, map making, navigation, and military practices. It was first used in the social sciences as a metaphor describing a form of multiple operationalism or convergent validation (Campbell 1956), and it was used to describe multiple data-collection technologies designed to measure a single concept or construct. Denzin introduced an additional metaphor, lines of action, which characterizes the use of multiple data-collection technologies, theories, researchers, methodologies, or combinations of these four categories of research activities (1978: 292). Triangulation as a method is restricted to the use of multiple data-gathering techniques to investigate the same phenomenon. This is what is required in future fashion/dress studies. Some examples of triangulation are presented throughout this book.

THE INTEGRATION OF QUALITATIVE AND QUANTITATIVE METHODS

While many qualitative researchers do not believe that one can analyze human experiences quantitatively, the most ideal methodology would be the integration of the qualitative and the quantitative methods.

Certain types of social research problems call for specific approaches (Creswell 2003). A research problem is an issue or concern that needs to be addressed. For example, if the problem is identifying factors that influence an outcome, then a quantitative approach is best. It is the best approach to use to test a theory or explanation. On the other hand, if a concept or phenomenon needs to be understood because little research has been done on it, then it merits a qualitative approach, which is exploratory and is useful when the researcher does not know the important variables to examine. This type of approach may be needed because the topic is new, the topic has never been addressed with a certain sample or group, or existing theories do not apply with the particular sample or group under study.

A mixed methods design is useful to capture the best of both quantitative and qualitative approaches. For example, you may want to both generalize the findings to a population and develop a detailed view of the meaning of a phenomenon or concept for individuals (Thompson 2002).

As explained earlier in the previous chapters, quantitative research can easily be distinguished from qualitative research in terms of their results. In quantitative research, the results are presented as quantities or statistical numbers. Researchers often use large, representative samples from which generalizations can be made regarding population parameters (Neuman 2000). Their research methods are questionnaires that have questions with multiple choice or yes/no answers that are converted into numerics, and they can be easily administered to large samples. An unbiased sample, which is the best way to obtain data that can be generalized to a population, is used. In contrast, in qualitative research, there are trends and themes that are described in words. The researchers emphasize the collection of in-depth information obtained from small samples without regard to generalizability to a population. Such information is frequently collected through extensive one-on-one interviews with participants. The intention is not to make generalizations to a population and therefore, the researchers strive for purposive samples. Individuals are purposively selected because they are likely to be good sources of information. Qualitative-oriented researchers take an in-depth look at their participants through intensive interviews, open-ended questionnaires, observations, and so on. Self-reports can be difficult to interpret while attempting to identify causal variables. Participants may not tell the truth about certain aspects of their behavior; also, they may not have the self-insights to understand why they do what they do. It is the job of a researcher to elicit information on possible causation and make the participants aware of their behavior and enable them to verbalize their feelings and their actions (Flick 1998).

There are some universals that should apply to all qualitative research methods, which should be evaluated on the same overall basis as other research, that is, according to whether it makes a substantive contribution to empirical knowledge and/or advances theory (Collins 1988; Marshall and Rossman 1999). Qualitative research can achieve this in multiple ways: it can provide new data or replicate previous studies within a different time and/or space frame; it gives voices to those not heard before, such as the youths in deviant fashion subcultures; it studies groups that are difficult to access and new fashion phenomena that are emerging; it can advance new theories of fashion or amend previously accepted ones. Consequently, qualitative research is vastly different from purely quantitative methods, but it can provide data and raise questions that no quantitative methods can generate partly because it allows for the emergence of unexpected phenomena.

CONCLUSION

The choice of one's research method depends on the researcher's own personal training and experiences. An individual trained in technical, scientific writing, statistics, and computerized statistical programs who is also familiar with quantitative journals in the library would most likely choose the quantitative design. The qualitative approach incorporates more of a literary form of writing and experience in conducting open-ended interviews and observations. The mixed methods researcher needs to be familiar with both quantitative and qualitative research, and he or she also needs an understanding of the rationales for combining both forms of data so that they can be articulated in a proposal.

GUIDE TO FURTHER READING

Baddeley, Gavin (2002), *Goth Chic: A Connoisseur's Guide to Dark Culture,* edited by Paul A. Woods, London: Plexus Publishing.

Breward, Christopher, and David Gilbert (eds.) (2006), *Fashion's World Cities,* Oxford, UK: Berg.

Chen, Tina Mai (2005), "Dressing for the Party: Clothing, Citizenship and Gender Formation in Mao's China," in Valerie Steele (ed.), *Fashion Theory: The Journal of Dress, Body and Culture,* 5/2: 143–71, Oxford, UK: Berg.

Clandinin, D. Jean, and Michael Connelly (2000), *Narrative Inquiry: Experience and Story in Qualitative Research,* San Francisco: Jossey-Bass.

Garfinkel, Harold (1973), *Studies in Ethnomethodology,* Malden, MA: Polity Press/Blackwell Publishing.

Hollander, Anne (1993), *Seeing through Clothes,* Berkeley: University of California Press.

Horwood, Catherine (2002), "Dressing like a Champion: Women's Tennis Wear in Interwar England," in Christopher Breward, Becky Conekin, and Caroline Cox (eds.), *The Englishness of English Dress,* pp. 45–60, Oxford, UK: Berg.

Ko, Dorothy (1997), "Bondage in Time: Footbinding and Fashion Theory," in Valerie Steele (ed.), *Fashion Theory: The Journal of Dress, Body and Culture,* 1/1: 3–27, Oxford, UK: Berg.

Paulicelli, Eugenia (2004), *Fashion under Fascism: Beyond the Black Shirt,* Oxford, UK: Berg.

Rocamora, Agnès (2001), "High Fashion and Pop Fashion: The Symbolic Production of Fashion in *Le Monde* and *The Guardian*," in Valerie Steele (ed.), *Fashion Theory: The Journal of Dress, Body and Culture,* 5/2: 123–42, Oxford, UK: Berg.

Spooner, Catherine (2004), *Fashioning Gothic Bodies,* Manchester, UK: Manchester University Press.

Tulloch, Carol (ed.) (2002), "Special Issue: Fashion and Photography," *Fashion Theory: The Journal of Dress, Body and Culture,* 6/1, Oxford, UK: Berg.

8 WRITING UP

Objectives

■ To understand each step of the final writing process.

■ To understand that each research method has different ways to write.

■ To identify the necessary and required components in a research paper.

■ To recognize the importance of references.

After completing the process of data collection in your research, you will probably write a paper or a report about your research project. Writing is a skilled craft, and that craft can be improved by writing, editing, and rewriting several times. This chapter introduces students who are not experienced in writing a research paper to the process of writing and what needs to be included in the paper and in what sequence. While a style of writing depends on your readers, clear and concise writing and avoiding all unnecessary jargon from any particular social scientific discipline are the best tactics. It is not necessary to use difficult vocabularies. Your paper has to be readable and comprehensible. Some basic guidelines for writing formal academic papers or reports are covered in this chapter.

The choice of your research method determines the style of your paper. For instance, for an ethnographic paper, you write what you observed, noting how people behaved and what they said. Your findings are often illustrated by specific observations, which can be summarized in your field notes. Sometimes, your field notes and interview notes are quoted directly and sometimes, they are incorporated into the text of your paper. People you talk to, places and cities you visit usually remain anonymous, and you should use fictitious names to avoid any presumptions in the minds of readers. In a quantitative research, graphs, charts, and tables are often included in findings.

After completing your paper, you can disseminate it to appropriate audiences so that you can get feedback, which may be useful for your future research.

THE STRUCTURE OF A RESEARCH PAPER

Major sections and components of standard social scientific reports are described. Your paper needs a structure with major headings and subheadings. A basic paper includes a title, abstract of the paper, introduction, literature review, methods used in research, findings, and conclusion. Your goal is to answer in writing, in a logical and coherent way, the same questions you have been asking about the text as you read. Refer back to the questions you are answering as you write. They can serve as a guide in determining which information you need to make your point and which is extraneous. Keeping your key questions in mind as you write and revise will keep you from wandering.

TITLE

The title usually appears on a title page with author information, such as the name and the affiliation. You should come up with a good title. Some come up with a title before starting a paper while others think of the title after or during the process of writing the paper. You need a good descriptive title that would attract readers. Good titles are self-explanatory and tell much about your research. The title gives readers an idea about your work so it should have the key words of your research. There is often the broad main title and a subheading describing the main title that is more specific and narrow than the main title. For example, *The Culture of Clothing: Dress and Fashion in the Ancien Regime* (Roche 1994) or "Ethnic Minimalism: A Strand of 1990s British Fashion Identity Explored via a Contextual Analysis of Designs by Shirin Guild" (Haye 2000), which has a very detailed subheading.

ABSTRACT

An abstract is a brief description or a summary of the paper/report. It describes the research problem/question/hypothesis, methods, sample, results, and conclusions of your study, and it should contain only ideas or information discussed in the body of the paper. Abstracts are found in the beginning of a paper immediately below the title. An abstract is always included in a journal article rather than in a book. Writing a concise and precise abstract is important since readers decide whether or not to continue reading the paper based on the abstract. If you are writing a paper for your class, you probably do not have to include an abstract.

INTRODUCTION

An introduction consists of basic research questions, key terms, and research focus. Scholarly papers and reports must begin with a formal introduction that cites literature. The introduction should state why the research problem/hypothesis is important and worth studying. It provides an overview of what has been said about the topic in the literature. You need to explain how your study differs from others that have already been reported. It is important to indicate the type of writing that will follow after the introduction, such as a descriptive/ethnographical report or a statistical survey analysis. The introduction should end with a statement describing your specific research objectives or hypothesis. The first opening sentence in the introduction is crucial and, therefore, needs to be interesting since it can either entice or lose readers.

LITERATURE REVIEW

As indicated in Chapter 2, "Research Process," a detailed examination of the past research literature relevant to your research topic is called a literature review. This is a process that every researcher goes through before conducting his or her own research. The literature review gives a comprehensive review of previous works on the general and specific topics considered in your paper. It should include references to classic works related to the investigation and should also include recent studies to show that you are up-to-date. The more thorough the literature review, the more solid the research paper's foundation becomes. It is like having a dialogue with other researchers, and you may want to challenge previously accepted ideas or findings. Without the literature review, your paper is not considered academic or scholarly. Keep in mind that writing only about your research is not sufficient in an academic paper.

RESEARCH DESIGN AND METHODOLOGY

After the literature review comes the methodology section. This is a comprehensive description of how the researchers gathered data and analyzed these data. You need to inform the readers how your research was accomplished, through which process. What do the data consist of and how were the data collected and analyzed? This section of the paper should describe the research methods for social science research. For a historical approach, library research is obvious with citations and sources. If it was a questionnaire, you explain how the respondents were selected, how many responded, and how many failed to respond. If demographic information has been collected, it should also be described here. It is essential to give an overview of how the questionnaire was developed, including a brief description of tryouts and item analysis, if any. If the actual questionnaire will be included in the paper/report, either as a figure or an appendix, the writer is obliged to describe it only briefly. If it is not included, the writer should describe the questionnaire in more detail and, at an absolute minimum, should indicate how many items there were in each section of the questionnaire and their form, such as open-ended or closed-ended questions. It is a good idea to provide sample items if the whole questionnaire is not included in the report. Describe when and how the questionnaires were distributed and collected or returned. If informed consent was obtained, it is important to mention this fact (see Chapter 2, "Research Process," about the Institutional Review Board).

While many researchers either omit or make this section very brief, it is very important to clearly state your research methods and the processes you used to conduct your research. These need to be specific and clear. The purpose is to allow anyone who is interested in repeating your research using the same methods to do so. Explain who your research subjects were, how they are selected, how many were in your study, how many turned down your request, and how they were informed about your research. Then you need to identify the nature of the data and explain how they were collected. The purpose of explaining your data collection process is to allow your readers to replicate a research study if they wish to. If it was an ethnographical study, the description of the research setting is important. For a quantitative study, you must indicate clearly where you got your raw data from.

FINDINGS AND RESULTS/ANALYSIS

In this section, information uncovered during the research process is presented. Findings are the data, and results are the interpretation/analysis of the data. There are different ways to present results from quantitative and qualitative research. In a quantitative paper, findings and results are the same, and the findings present percentages and proportions of the data in the form of charts, tables, and graphs as discussed in Chapter 4, "Survey Methods." But in the case of qualitative research, there are several options that are available for writing about the findings and results of the data, which are often treated separately. The findings or results section is not as easily explained. For example, in qualitative research, the analysis section often follows the methods section, or data are presented throughout their analysis in order to demonstrate and document various patterns and observations. Sections of qualitative writings are often organized according to conceptual subheadings that were found during research.

DISCUSSION/IMPLICATIONS/CONCLUSION

The discussion section amounts to reiteration and elaboration of key points and suggestions about how the findings fit into the existing literature on the topical study area. You must remember that no research is perfect, absolute, or definitive so you can discuss some of the weaknesses found or the limitations of your research methodology. Everyone is making a contribution in the research community or in the fashion/dress studies community as a scholar or a researcher. Therefore, other researchers may find your research worthwhile and meaningful, and they will refer to your study in their research. After completing a research project, the researchers realize that they have gained greater knowledge and insight into the phenomenon investigated. At the same time, you realize what needs to be studied further.

REFERENCES/BIBLIOGRAPHY AND NOTES

When writing a research paper, you must follow a special set of formal conventions for documentation. For textual analysis, it is usually sufficient to indicate in the first reference only the publication date of the text you are using. Thereafter, you may document quotations with the author's last name and appropriate page number. When referring to an idea or argument found more generally throughout the text, you should include the author's name alone in one of your own sentences.

There are two ways to reference materials you used in your research: notes and source references. In the social sciences, source references are more often used for documenting statements made in the text, and notes generally give further explanation to the text rather than cite source references. Source references are identified by the last name of a reference author, the date of publication, and in the case of a direct quotation, the page from which the quote has been taken. All of the works cited in your paper must be in the bibliography pages. A bibliography at the very end of your paper or book allows the readers to see whether you are aware of recent as well as classic seminal works in your area of expertise. By looking at your list, readers can see the direction of your research.

There are various writing style guides for different disciplines, such as APA (American Psychological Association), MLA (Modern Language Association), CMS (*The Chicago Manual of Style*), Harvard, CGOS (Columbia Guide to Online Style), and CBE (Council of Biology Editors). The style that is used in social science publications and historical journals is CMS, which is also applicable to fashion and dress studies.

DISSEMINATING A RESEARCH PAPER

Just as clothes designed by designers are manufactured, transformed into fashion, and then disseminated as fashion, your research once completed can also be disseminated at professional conferences and possibly as publications. If you are a student, you spend a considerable number of weeks and sometimes even months writing your paper, so you would want to expose your research results to the public and to those who may be interested in your research questions as well as your findings. Similarly, research is often done for an MA/MS thesis or a PhD dissertation.

CONCLUSION

After you complete your data collection, you will sit down and write your paper or book so that others can read about your research project. There are basic components that any research paper should have, so make sure you cover them in your paper. Your paper needs to be readable and to contain reference materials.

GUIDE TO FURTHER READING

Coyle, William, and Joe Law (2009), *Research Papers,* Englewood Cliffs, NJ: Longman.

Goldenberg, Phyllis (2004), *Writing a Research Paper: A Step-by-Step Approach,* New York: William H. Sadlier.

Lester, James D. (2006), *Writing Research Papers in the Social Sciences,* Englewood Cliffs, NJ: Longman.

Lester, James D. (2009), *Writing Research Papers,* Englewood Cliffs, NJ: Longman.

Stebbins, Robert Alan (2001), *Exploratory Research in the Social Sciences (Qualitative Research Methods),* London: Sage Publications.

CONCLUSION: FUTURE OPPORTUNITIES AND DIRECTIONS IN FASHION/DRESS STUDIES

Objectives

■ To explore the future opportunities of fashion/dress studies research.

■ To recognize the role and the placement of fashion in postmodern times.

■ To re-examine the idea of fashion as a Western/non-Western concept.

■ To understand the importance of bridging the gap between scholars and practitioners.

Fashion as a business is an enormous industry, and consumers in general, especially women, like clothes, and they enjoy shopping for clothes. Cyclical changes in the selection of clothes in department stores and boutiques never ceases to fascinate us. New styles and designs are introduced every season so that we can refresh our wardrobe. While fashion surrounds us, fashion/dress studies requires us to look at it from a scholarly perspective. However, academics are fashion consumers as well, and it does not mean we need to keep academics and industry practitioners as separate groups of people as if there were no overlaps between the two. The gap between the two needs to be filled as both can learn from the other.

As explained earlier in this book, fashion as a research topic is still considered very marginal, on the periphery of any intellectual discussions. We need the legitimation of the research community as well as their recognition so that more financial support becomes available to the scholars who wish to study fashion/dress. Therefore, it is the responsibility of fashion/dress scholars to elevate the importance as well as the interests of the topic in academia. We need to make sure that fashion/dress studies continues to prosper with more research-funding opportunities.

Furthermore, we live in a new historical phase called a postmodern society, with every idea and every phenomenon taking a postmodern turn. Fashion is known as a modern phenomenon, but fashion can also be analyzed from a postmodern perspective. Fashion is often considered to be a Western concept, but that idea can be revisited in today's postmodern times.

PLACING FASHION IN POSTMODERN TIMES

There are signs of cultural turmoil everywhere. A broad social and cultural shift is taking place, and the concept of the "postmodern" captures at least certain aspects of this transformation. The transition from modernity to postmodernity is a consequence of social, political, and cultural changes in the relationships between different social groups. Modernity presumes the existence of clear distinctions between different types and genres of aesthetic and stylistic endeavors while postmodernity no longer recognizes these categories as legitimate or even necessary. Fashion emphasizes images and incessant change, and this constitutes the epitome of a postmodernist cultural form. Postmodernity is difficult to characterize because of its preoccupation with ambiguity and contradiction. It has no fixed meanings and often has multiple meanings, and these meanings are unstable, contradictory, and incessantly changing. One of the major characteristics of a postmodern phenomenon is the breakdown of boundaries and categories. Whatever used to be classified as a group becomes gradually meaningless.

Therefore, fashion/dress scholars need to shift their focus slightly to make the postmodern interpretation of fashion, which is different from the modern interpretation that many have made since the clothing distinctions, such as menswear/womenswear, high fashion/popular fashion, outerwear/innerwear, are already beginning to collapse. The rules of the clothing system are also flexible. Today's youths in the industrialized countries no longer follow the traditional sartorial conventions as to how clothes should look, what they need to be made out of, or how they should be worn. Postmodern consumers are extremely creative, and thus the lines that used to be clearly drawn between fashion professionals, such as designers and stylists, and consumers are also blurry. We as researchers need to be aware of these changes in the world of fashion.

No one explains the meaning of fashion in a postmodern society better than Crane who argues that we see a shift from class fashion to consumer fashion (2000), especially in the West. In postmodern cultures, consumption is conceptualized as a form of role playing, as consumers seek to project conceptions of identity that are continually evolving. In contemporary Western society, social class is less evident and important in one's self-image and identity in society than before. Style differentiation no longer distinguishes social classes. There is a great deal of interclass and intraclass mobility.

Social identity that used to be based on the economic and political sphere is now based on something outside. According to Crane (2000: 11), "[T]he consumption of cultural goods, such as fashionable clothing, performs an increasingly important role in the construction of personal identity, while the satisfaction of material needs and the emulation of superior classes are secondary." One's style of dress conveys an initial and continuing impression-making image. The variety of lifestyles available in contemporary society liberates the individual from tradition and enables him or her to make choices that create a meaningful self-identity (Giddens 1991).

Contexts in which fashion/dress is placed, rather than the contents, that is, the clothing itself, are what we need to focus on. Therefore, material clothing itself is less important than the frames that are used to sell it, which can be used in turn to sell licensed products (Crane 2000: 15). Consumers are no longer perceived as "cultural dopes" or "fashion victims" who imitate fashion leaders but as people selecting styles on the basis of their perceptions of their own identities and lifestyles. Postmodern consumers are active producers of fashion. A style is a reflection of an individual identity since each individual is treated as a unique being in postmodern thinking. Fashion is presented as a choice rather than a mandate. The consumer is expected to "construct" an individualized appearance from a variety of options. A collection of materials drawn from many sources, clothing styles have different meanings for different social groups.

As Davis (1992) points out, fashion expresses individual identity. In postmodern times, individuals have multiple identities with different roles to perform, and therefore, they choose their identification from the numerous ranges of images and styles. Traditional ways of collective classifications and groupings, such as class, gender, race, and place, are gradually being replaced by individual and personal consumer identities. The members of postmodern societies demonstrate a fragmented, heterogeneous, and individualistic stylistic identification (Muggleton 2000).

SCHOLARS VERSUS PRACTITIONERS

There is a clear separation between scholars and practitioners who work in the industry, but we need to close the gap so that both can benefit from the other. There are more and more attempts to bridge the link between academia and the industry, which used to be completely separate and divided. Research is not only for academics, and the industry practitioners can benefit from academic research on fashion/dress to improve their business opportunities and apply it to their practical, day-to-day operations, while the scholars and researchers can gain much from the practitioners and can use their experiences for their empirical case studies. After all, many fashion/dress scholars observe, survey, and interview designers, buyers, marketers, and journalists in the industry as their research subjects.

There is also a possibility of teaching students in fashion schools the theories of fashion/dress. Some mistakenly equate fashion/dress studies with fashion design classes. Fashion design classes are often hands-on classes where students learn the garment constructions, sewing techniques, and making inspiration boards, while fashion studies are more theory-oriented and academic.

Else Skjold, a graduate student in Sweden, in her unpublished PhD dissertation entitled "Fashion Research at Design Schools," raises a thought-provoking and a very important question: Do fashion design students need to study fashion theories?[1] She visited a number of fashion schools in Europe and the United States and interviewed fashion scholars and theorists. Fashion designers are required to be knowledge workers rather than only hands-on clothing production experts. She explores positive ways in which fashion research can be integrated in fashion design education using Designskolen Kolding (DK) in Sweden as a case study. The decision was made by the Swedish Ministry of Culture in the 1980s to change the name of design education from "arts and crafts schools" to "design schools" (2008: 15), which can affect and change people's perception of the schools. The debate concerning research as such versus practice-based training has caused a very heated public debate over the past few years, according to Skjold (2008).

Some of Skjold's key questions are as follows (2008: 25): (1) How is fashion research implemented in a design school? (2) How can fashion research create possibilities in education in relation to the fashion industry? (3) How to strengthen already existing competencies through research? (4) How to communicate research internally within an institution?

Fashion design students are trained to be successful designers in the industry. Some may work for apparel companies as commercial designers, and others may eventually set up their own brands and become their own bosses. While in school, they learn to drape, cut patterns, draft paper patterns, and learn basic sewing techniques. Is there a place for fashion theory? Do they need to know Simmel, Veblen, Crane, or Muggleton? Is it simply a waste of time?

I write this from my own experience because before I became a sociologist, I studied fashion design hoping to become a professional designer. At the time I knew nothing about the trickle-down theory of fashion or the research process. We were taught the technical aspects of fashion design, and I was blindly learning them. By the time I was writing a doctoral dissertation on the sociology of fashion, I had read the major classical and contemporary theories of fashion. Had I known them when I was studying to be a designer, my perspectives on fashion would have been different and what I actually designed would have been more carefully executed with specific social and cultural statements or messages.

RESEARCH FUNDING OPPORTUNITIES

Unlike many other research areas and topics considered socially significant, fashion as a topic is less likely to receive research funding. Many organizations do not see the necessity in funding such a topic, which is another indication of the devaluation of fashion as a research topic. Therefore, by bridging the divide between academia and the industry, the latter may be able to fund research studies on fashion and dress.

Research is needed to create and maintain a fashion culture. While Paris, New York, Milan, and London are the four established fashion cities that have a solid foundation of a fashion culture, there are many other cities in the world that are making an attempt to create the same kind of fashion culture. It will be beneficial not only for the local economy but for the world economy if fashion as an industry as well as a system can further be investigated in social sciences through funding from corporations.

FASHION AS A UNIVERSAL/GLOBAL CONCEPT

Dress from non-Western cultures was collected in Europe from the late sixteenth century onward as visual evidence of the existence of exotic, mysterious peoples. Taylor (2004: 67) explains that by the late nineteenth century the collection and examination of garments and body ornaments was included within the emerging academic discipline of anthropology, and they were treated as cultural artifacts, such as tools or weapons. Still today, studies and museum collections on ethnic dress are limited.

While Cannon (1998) argues that fashion is found in traditional cultures as well, fashion was often believed to be a Western concept and phenomenon. Some of the classical theorists, such as J. C. Flugel (1930) and Ferdinand Toennies (1961 [1909]), have argued that fashion originated in the West and is a Western product. Toennies explained the differences between fixed costume found in simple societies and modish costume found in complex societies, implying that costumes that change frequently exist only in the civilized West (1961 [1909]). Such a statement seems to confirm the idea that fashion first started in the West.

Since the 1980s, that has been much debated among contemporary writers (Cannon 1998; Craik 1994), and some argued that fashion can be found even in ethnic dress, such as Japanese kimono or Indian sari. It depends on how one defines fashion. Once we can come up with a clear definition of fashion/dress, we can then apply it to non-Western fashion/dress.

In the study of costume by European and American scholars, fashion and Western dress have enjoyed privileged positions (Baizerman, Eicher, and Cerny 2008: 123). They pay less attention to ethnic dress of non-Western cultures. We need to focus more on cultural pluralism and multiculturalism in the aspects of dress and fashion studies and conduct more in-depth research on ethnic fashion/dress so that we can acquire facts and evidence to come up with convincing findings. Studies of ethnic dress are often ethnographical, which consumes much time and money. Furthermore, museums across the United States and Europe need to collect and conserve ethnic costumes so that they can be used in material culture studies.

Baizerman, Eicher, and Cerny (2008) argue that dress has been studied from an ethnocentric/Eurocentric point of view. European aesthetic standards and European perceptions of clothing were applied when representing non-European modes. They make a provocative yet convincing statement by referring to "Social Darwinism." Darwin's theory of evolution justifies the colonial attitude of the Euro-American to other people of the world. Dress was touted as a visible manifestation of the civilized state of being, of cultural superiority where advancement was defined in terms of superior economic development and global dominance. Modifying dress practices of the colonized to parallel those of the West was seen as a way of extending civilization (Baizerman, Eicher, and Cerny 2008: 124).

As discussed in the "Introduction" section of this book, Eurocentric assumptions are found even in the terminology usage. Baizerman, Eicher, and Cerny (2008) also try to come up with the best term for non-Western dress. The term they eventually proposed is either "regional dress" or "ethnic dress." Their study informs us of the significance of using the correct or the most appropriate term and also the importance of understanding the cultural biases and prejudice included in these terms so that the conclusions of any research are as objective as they can be. It is always wise to start with definitions of the terms and concepts we study so that we as researchers can make sure and confirm to ourselves that we are accurately understanding them.

The symposium entitled "Cultural Transfer: Orientalism and Occidentalism in Fashion"[2] took place at the University of Potsdam in November 2009 where fashion/dress scholars presented papers on the integration of the West and the East in fashion, the historical Oriental influences on Western fashion and vice versa. More academic conferences with such endeavors need to be organized so that fashion/dress scholars become more aware of the fact that fashion was not and is not simply a Western idea.

Furthermore, Paulicelli and Clark edited a book entitled *The Fabric of Cultures: Fashion, Identity, Globalization* (2008), which explores the relationships of fashion to identity, the global and the local, and the interrelations of cultures from multidisciplinary perspectives. It includes articles on Indian cinema costume (Tu 2008), fashion in Soviet Russia in the 1950s and 1960s (Gurova 2008), and youth fashion in Vietnam (Leshkowich 2008), among others.

It is about time that we treat fashion as a global concept transcending not only disciplinary boundaries but also cultural boundaries.

CONCLUSION

Fashion/dress studies is recent in its origin so there are countless opportunities and directions for scholars to take. As time changes, fashion changes since fashion is a reflection of the current ideology of a society. Fashion/dress scholars need to have more dialogue with fellow colleagues and students about where, how, and to whom to teach fashion/dress theories. The gap between scholars and practitioners in the industry can be filled so that both sides benefit from the other's knowledge, expertise, and experiences. Academic institutions, such as colleges and universities, academic publishers, conference organizers and sponsors, must work together to make fashion/dress studies a legitimate field of research.

GUIDE TO FURTHER READING

Baizerman, Suzanne, Joanne B. Eicher, and Catherine Cerny (2008), "Eurocentrism in the Study of Ethnic Dress," in Joanne B. Eicher, Sandra Lee Evenson, and Hazel A. Lutz (eds.), *The Visible Self: Global Perspectives on Dress, Culture, and Society,* pp. 123–32, New York: Fairchild Publications.

Cannon, Aubrey (1998), "The Cultural and Historical Contexts of Fashion," in Sandra Niessen and Anne Bryden (eds.), *Consuming Fashion: Adorning the Transnational Body,* pp. 23–38, Oxford, UK: Berg.

Craik, Jennifer (1994), *The Face of Fashion,* London: Routledge.

Flugel, J. C. (1930), *The Psychology of Clothes,* London: Hogarth.

Lyotard, Jean-François (1984), *The Postmodern Condition,* Minneapolis: University of Minnesota Press.

Skjold, Else (2008), "Fashion Research at Design Schools," unpublished PhD dissertation, Designskolen Kolding, Jutland, Sweden.

Skov, Lise (1996, August), "Fashion Trends, Japonisme and Postmodernism," *Theory, Culture and Society,* 13/3: 129–51.

Toennies, Ferdinand (1961 [1909]), *Custom: An Essay on Social Codes,* trans. A. F. Borenstein, New York: Free Press.

Tseëlon, Efrat (1994), "Fashion and Signification in Baudrillard," in Douglas Kellner (ed.), *Baudrillard: A Critical Reader,* pp. 119–32, Oxford, UK: Basil Blackwell.

NOTES

Introduction

1. Throughout this book, I use "fashion" and "dress" side by side since I am not simply talking about studies on fashion but also studies on dress, which consists of material clothing as well as any objects and practices that are related to adornment.
2. *Fashion Foundations: Early Writings on Fashion and Dress* (2003), written by Kim K. P. Johnson, Susan J. Torntore, and Joanne B. Eicher, is very helpful in understanding fashion/dress–related research studies in different chronological times. The book includes excerpts taken from early writings between 1575 and 1940 by costume historians, economists, psychologists, sociologists, feminists, and social activists.
3. Michael Carter's book *Fashion Classics from Carlyle to Barthes* (2003) gives an overview of the writings by eight classical fashion theorists: Thomas Carlyle, J. C. Flugel, Thornstein Veblen, Georg Simmel, Herbert Spencer, A. L. Kroeber, James Laver, and Roland Barthes. They laid the foundation for and influenced the conceptual and the theoretical understanding and interpretation of contemporary clothing and fashion. I would also add William Graham Sumner, Ferdinand Toennies, and Gabriel Tarde to this list of those who have made a theoretical contribution to fashion/dress studies.
4. If you wish to explore further each of the classical theorists mentioned above, it is highly recommended that you read their original texts indicated in the bibliography at the end of this book.
5. Erling Persson is the founder of a major Swedish clothing company, H&M (Hennes & Mauritz AB), that was established in 1947. It has 1,800 stores in 35 countries (www.hm.com).

Chapter 1: Theory and Practice

1. There is a clear difference between making theoretical generalizations and stereotyping. Students often mistake social scientific theorizing as stereotyping. Social science is based on solid research, and it challenges people's false assumptions and taken-for-granted preconceptions. Stereotyping simply emerges from one's speculations and guesswork, and it is often based on prejudice and biases that stem from someone's personal experiences.
2. These men were the first members of the Chicago School where researchers specialized in urban sociology using the ethnographical method. They are known for the development of the symbolic interactionist approach. The basic premise of the theory is that human behavior is shaped by social structures and physical environment factors.

Chapter 2: Research Process

1. Phenomenology, which was started by Edmund Husserl (1859–1938), a German scholar, in the early twentieth century, is a philosophy or a method of inquiry based on the premise that reality consists of objects and events as they are perceived in human consciousness. It emphasizes the first-person viewpoint and subjectivity. See more in *Introduction to Phenomenology* (1999) by Robert Sokolowski.

2. Epistemology studies the nature, origin, and limits of knowledge.
3. Since there is often a strong connection between a researcher and the topic he or she selects, many think that I am a fan of the Japanese designers in Paris. Fortunately or unfortunately, that is not true. I am interested in their work as a researcher, but I do not wear their clothes.
4. See Chapter 4, "Survey Methods," for descriptions. One of the major differences between probability and nonprobability sampling is that the former involves random sampling while the latter does not. See more in *Sampling* (2002) by Steven K. Thompson.

Chapter 3: Ethnography

1. Hermeneutics is the theory of interpretation. In sociology in particular, it means the interpretation of social events by analyzing the meanings of the human participants and their culture. It is not only people's social behavior that needs attention but also the context in which it belongs.
2. In 1919, Alfred Kroeber measured the illustrations of women's dress in fashion plates that were idealized depictions of women's clothing styles. Edward Sapir wrote an article on "Fashion" and Ruth Benedict wrote one on "Dress" for *The Encyclopedia of the Social Sciences* in 1931.
3. Herbert Blumer published an important article entitled "Fashion: From Class Differentiation to Collective Selection" in *The Sociological Quarterly* in 1969.
4. Postmodernity or postmodern condition is a state of society that comes after modernity, and it is sometimes called "late capitalism." No one knows exactly when it started. Some scholars claim that modernity ended at the end of the twentieth century, and it was replaced by postmodernity. One of the characteristics of a postmodern phenomenon is the breakdown of traditional barriers. See more in *The Postmodern Condition* (1984) by Jean-François Lyotard.
5. The term "Hawthorne effect" was named after a manufacturing facility. Research was conducted to see whether the darkness or the lightness of the room that workers worked in had any impact on their productivity level. It turned out that the productivity level increased not due to any environmental conditions, but it was the researchers' interest in the workers that improved their productivity. When the research was over, productivity dropped, so knowing that they are part of research could change people's behavior.

Chapter 4: Survey Methods

1. A pilot study is a preliminary research and analysis conducted before the real study to assess the feasibility of the study. It pretests a research instrument such as a questionnaire or an interview schedule.
2. Rensis Likert (1903–1981), an American social scientist, developed the Likert scale that indicates the level of agreement/disagreement to a given statement in questionnaires.
3. There are many graphics software programs for drawing graphs. If you have Microsoft Office installed on your PC, you can draw charts and graphs with Microsoft Excel, which is usually included in the package.
4. For further details, see *Inside Subculture: The Postmodern Meaning of Style* (2000) by David Muggleton.
5. For further details, see "Appendix 2: Interview Schedules; Questionnaire for Focus Groups Interview Schedule," pp. 255–9, in *Fashion and Its Social Agendas: Class, Gender, and Identity in Clothing* (2000) by Diana Crane. Also see Paul Hodkinson's study on Goth subculture (2002), which is another research that used questionnaires. Self-completion questionnaires were distributed at the Whitby Gothic Weekend in October 1997. In order to gain some idea of typicality by garnering multichoice answers and short comments from a wider range of Goths, Hodkinson used the questionnaire sample of 112, which was, according to the author, not large enough to make any generalizations. Thus questionnaire data is treated as secondary relative to the other methods. The quantitative questionnaire results are found in "Appendix: Quantitative Questionnaire Results" (pp. 199–202).

6. For the entire interview schedule, see *The Japanese Revolution in Paris Fashion* (2004), pp. 173–4, by Yuniya Kawamura.

Chapter 5: Semiotics/Semiology

1. Strictly speaking, there are differences between semiotics and semiology, but it is not the intention of this book to examine these differences in detail. It was Charles Sanders Peirce (1839–1914) who first coined the term "semiotics" and viewed signs as part of an ongoing process of human action. But it was Ferdinand de Saussure (1857–1913) who made a major contribution to the discipline of semiology as part of the social sciences as explained in this chapter.
2. The English translations of the original publications by Saussure and Barthes are too complex for undergraduate students, so read some introductory books on semiology before you tackle the original ones. *Signs in Contemporary Culture: An Introduction to Semiotics* (1998) by Arthur Asa Berger and *Roland Barthes* (2003) by Graham Allen are recommended.
3. Lurie has a chapter, "I. Clothing as a Sign System" (pp. 3–36), in her book *The Language of Clothes* (2000 [1981]).

Conclusion: Future Opportunities and Directions in Fashion/Dress Studies

1. I currently teach sociology of fashion as a required course to students who major in accessories design at the Fashion Institute of Technology.
2. The symposium was organized by Gertrud Lehnert of Potsdam University and Gabriele Mentges of Dortmund University.

BIBLIOGRAPHY

Adler, Patricia, and Peter Adler (1998), "Observational Techniques," in Norman Denzin and Yvonna Lincoln (eds.), *Collecting and Interpreting Qualitative Materials,* pp. 79–109, Thousand Oaks, CA: Sage Publications.

Allen, Graham (2003), *Roland Barthes,* London: Routledge.

Amann, Elizabeth (2009), "Blonde Trouble: Women in Wigs in the Wake of Thermidor," in Valerie Steele (ed.), *Fashion Theory: The Journal of Dress, Body and Culture,* 13/3: 299–324, Oxford, UK: Berg.

Antick, Paul (2002), "Bloody Jumpers: Benetton and the Mechanics of Cultural Exclusion," in Carol Tulloch (ed.), Special Issue: Fashion and Photography, *Fashion Theory: The Journal of Dress, Body and Culture,* 6/1: 83–110, Oxford, UK: Berg.

Arnold, Janet (1977), *Pattern of Fashion: Englishwomen's Dresses and Their Construction,* London: Drama Publishing.

Arnold, Rebecca (1999), "Heroin Chic," in Valerie Steele (ed.), *Fashion Theory: The Journal of Dress, Body and Culture,* 3/3: 279–96, Oxford, UK: Berg.

Arnold, Rebecca (2000), "Luxury and Restraint: Minimalism in 1990s Fashion," in Nicola White and Ian Griffiths (eds.), *The Fashion Business: Theory, Practice, Image,* pp. 167–81, Oxford, UK: Berg.

Arnold, Rebecca (2002), "Looking American: Louise Dahl-Wolfe's Fashion Photographs of the 1930s and 1940s," in Carol Tulloch (ed.), Special Issue: Fashion and Photography, *Fashion Theory: The Journal of Dress, Body and Culture,* 6/1: 46–60, Oxford, UK: Berg.

Aspers, Patrik (2001), *Markets in Fashion: A Phenomenological Approach,* Stockholm, Sweden: City University Press.

Aspers, Patrik (2006, September), "Contextual Knowledge," in Patrik Aspers and Lise Skov (eds.), *Current Sociology,* 54/5: 745–63, Thousand Oaks, CA: Sage Publications.

Babbie, Earl (1998), *The Practice of Social Research,* Belmont, CA: Wadsworth Publishing.

Baddeley, Gavin (2002), *Goth Chic: A Connoisseur's Guide to Dark Culture,* edited by Paul A. Woods, London: Plexus Publishing.

Baizerman, Suzanne, Joanne B. Eicher, and Catherine Cerny (2008), "Eurocentrism in the Study of Ethnic Dress," in Joanne B. Eicher, Sandra Lee Evenson, and Hazel A. Lutz (eds.), *The Visible Self: Global Perspectives on Dress, Culture, and Society,* pp. 123–32, New York: Fairchild Publications.

Barnard, Malcolm (1996), *Fashion as Communication,* London: Routledge.

Barnard, Malcolm (2007a), "Introduction," in Malcolm Barnard (ed.), *Fashion Theory: A Reader,* pp. 1–14, London: Routledge.

Barnard, Malcolm (ed.) (2007b), *Fashion Theory: A Reader,* London: Routledge.

Barnes, Ruth, and Joanne B. Eicher (eds.) (1992), *Dress and Gender: Making and Meaning in Cultural Context,* Oxford, UK: Berg.

Barthes, Roland (1972), *Mythologies,* trans. Annette Lavers, New York: Farrar, Straus and Giroux.

Barthes, Roland (1977), *Elements of Semiology,* trans. Annette Lavers and Colin Smith, New York: Hill and Wang.

Barthes, Roland (1990), *The Fashion System,* trans. Matthew Ward and Richard Howard, Berkeley: University of California Press.

Barthes, Roland (2006), *The Language of Fashion,* Oxford, UK: Berg.

Baudrillard, Jean (1972), *For a Critique of the Political Economy of the Sign,* trans. Charles Levin, St. Louis, MO: Telos Press.

Beard, Alice (2002), "'Put in Just for Pictures': Fashion Editorial and the Composite Image in *Nova* 1965–1975," in Carol Tulloch (ed.), Special Issue: Fashion and Photography, *Fashion Theory: The Journal of Dress, Body and Culture,* 6/1: 25–44, Oxford, UK: Berg.

Benedict, Ruth (1931), "Dress," *Encyclopedia of the Social Sciences,* Vol. 5, pp. 235–7, London: Macmillan.

Berger, Arthur Asa (1992), *Reading Matter: Multidisciplinary Perspectives on Material Culture,* New Brunswick, NJ: Transaction Publishers.

Berger, Arthur Asa (1998), *Signs in Contemporary Culture: An Introduction to Semiotics,* Salem, WI: Sheffield Publishing.

Berger, Peter L., and Thomas Luckmann (1966), *The Social Construction of Reality,* New York: Anchor Books.

Biddle-Perry, G. (2005), "'Bury Me in Purple Lurex': Promoting a New Dynamic between Fashion and Oral History," *Oral History Society,* 33/1: 88–92, Hertfordshire, UK: Oral History.

Black, Sandy, and Marilyn de Long (eds.) (2009–), *Fashion and Practice: The Journal of Design, Creative Process and the Fashion Industry,* Oxford, UK: Berg.

Blumer, Herbert (1969a), "Fashion: From Class Differentiation to Collective Selection," *The Sociological Quarterly,* 10/3: 275–91.

Blumer, Herbert (1969b), *Symbolic Interactionism: Perspective and Method,* Englewood Cliffs, NJ: Prentice-Hall.

Boer, Inge (2002), "Just a Fashion?: Cultural Cross-dressing and the Dynamics of Cross-cultural Representations," in Valerie Steele (ed.), *Fashion Theory: The Journal of Dress, Body and Culture,* 6/4: 421–40, Oxford, UK: Berg.

Bogardus, E. S. (1924), "Social Psychology of Fads," *Journal of Applied Sociology,* No. 8: 239–43.

Bordens, Kenneth, and Bruce Barrington Abbott (2007), *Research Design and Methods: A Process Approach,* New York: McGraw-Hill.

Boucher, François (1987 [1967]), *20,000 Years of Fashion: The History of Costume and Personal Adornment,* New York: Harry N. Abrams.

Brenninkmeyer, Ingrid (1963), *The Sociology of Fashion,* Köln-Oplanden, Germany: Westdeutscher Verlag.

Breward, Christopher (1995), *The Culture of Fashion: A New History of Fashionable Dress,* Manchester, UK: Manchester University Press.

Breward, Christopher (1998), "Cultures, Identities, Histories: Fashioning a Cultural Approach to Dress," in Anthea Javis (ed.), Special Issue: Methodology, *Fashion Theory: The Journal of Dress, Body and Culture,* 2/4: 301–14, Oxford, UK: Berg.

Breward, Christopher, Becky Conekin, and Caroline Cox (2002a), "Introduction: Dyed in the Wool English?," in Christopher Breward, Becky Conekin, and Caroline Cox (eds.), *The Englishness of English Dress,* pp. 1–14, Oxford, UK: Berg.

Breward, Christopher, Becky Conekin, and Caroline Cox (eds.) (2002b), *The Englishness of English Dress,* Oxford, UK: Berg.

Breward, Christopher, and David Gilbert (eds.) (2006), *Fashion's World Cities,* Oxford, UK: Berg.

Buck, Anne (1983), "Clothes in Fact and Fiction 1825–1865," *Costume,* No. 17: 89.

Burman, B. (ed.) (1999), *The Culture of Sewing: Gender, Consumption and Home Dressmaking,* Oxford, UK: Berg.

Buzzi, Stella, and Gibson, Pamela Church (eds.) (2001), *Fashion Cultures: Theories, Explorations, Analysis,* London: Routledge.

Calefato, Patrizia (1997), "Fashion and Worldliness: Imagery of the Clothed Body," in Valerie Steele (ed.), *Fashion Theory: The Journal of Dress, Body and Culture,* 1/1: 69–90, Oxford, UK: Berg.

Campbell, Donald (1956), *Leadership and Its Effects upon the Group,* Columbus: Ohio State University Press.

Cannon, Aubrey (1998), "The Cultural and Historical Contexts of Fashion," in Sandra Niessen and Anne Bryden (eds.), *Consuming Fashion: Adorning the Transnational Body,* pp. 23–38, Oxford, UK: Berg.

Carlyle, Thomas (2008 [1831]), *Sartor Resartus,* New York: Oxford University Press.

Carter, Michael (2003), *Fashion Classics from Carlyle to Barthes,* Oxford, UK: Berg.

Cheddie, Janice (2002), "The Politics of the First: The Emergence of the Black Model in the Civil Rights Era," in Carol Tulloch (ed.), Special Issue: Fashion and Photography, *Fashion Theory: The Journal of Dress, Body and Culture,* 6/1: 61–82, Oxford, UK: Berg.

Chen, Tina Mai (2005, June), "Dressing for the Party: Clothing, Citizenship and Gender Formation in Mao's China," in Valerie Steele (ed.), *Fashion Theory: The Journal of Dress, Body and Culture,* 5/2: 143–71, Oxford, UK: Berg.

Clandinin, D. Jean, and Michael Connelly (2000), *Narrative Inquiry: Experience and Story in Qualitative Research,* San Francisco: Jossey-Bass.

Clark, Hazel (1999), "The Cheung Sam: Issues of Fashion and Cultural Identity," in Valerie Steele and John Major (eds.), *China Chic: East Meets West,* pp. 155–65, New Haven, CT: Yale University Press.

Clark, Hazel (2000), *The Cheongsam,* Oxford, UK: Oxford University Press.

Clark, Hazel (2009), "Fashion 'China Style' in the Twenty-first Century," in Eugenia Paulicelli and Hazel Clark (eds.), *The Fabric of Cultures: Fashion, Identity, Globalization,* pp. 177–91, London: Routledge.

Clarke, Alison, and Daniel Miller (2002), "Fashion and Anxiety," in Valerie Steele (ed.), *Fashion Theory: The Journal of Dress, Body and Culture,* 6/2: 191–214, Oxford, UK: Berg.

Cohen, Noam (2009, August 24), "Wikipedia to Limit Changes to Articles on People," *The New York Times,* p. B1.

Collins, Randall (1988), *Theoretical Sociology,* San Diego, CA: Harcourt Brace Jovanovich.

Coyle, William, and Joe Law (2009), *Research Papers,* Englewood Cliffs, NJ: Longman.

Craik, Jennifer (1994), *The Face of Fashion,* London: Routledge.

Crane, Diana (2000), *Fashion and Its Social Agendas: Class, Gender, and Identity in Clothing,* Chicago: University of Chicago Press.

Creswell, John W. (2003), *Research Design: Qualitative, Quantitative, and Mixed Methods Approaches,* Thousand Oaks, CA: Sage Publications.

Csikszentmihalyi, Mihaly, and Eugene Rochberg-Halton (1981), *The Meaning of Things: Domestic Symbols and the Self,* Cambridge, UK: Cambridge University Press.

Cunningham, Patricia (2003), *Reforming Women's Fashion 1850–1920: Politics, Health, and Art,* Kent, OH: Kent State University Press.

Dalby, Liza (1983), *Geisha,* Berkeley: University of California Press.

Dalby, Liza (1998), *Kimono: Fashioning Culture,* New Haven, CT: Yale University Press.

Dale, Angela, Sara Arber, and Michael Procter (1988), *Doing Secondary Analysis,* Contemporary Social Research Series, London: Unwin Hyman.

Daly, M. Catherine (1999), "'Ah, A Real Kalabari Woman!': Reflexivity and the Conceptualization of Appearance," in Valerie Steele (ed.), *Fashion Theory: The Journal of Dress, Body and Culture,* 3/3: 343–62, Oxford, UK: Berg.

Davenport, Millia (1952), *A History of Costume,* London: Thames and Hudson.

Davis, Fred (1992), *Fashion, Culture, and Identity,* Chicago: University of Chicago Press.

Denzin, Norman (1978), *The Research Act,* New York: McGraw-Hill.

Duncan, Hugh Dalziel (1969), *Symbols and Social Theory,* Oxford, UK: Oxford University Press.

Eastop, Dinah (2005, July 26–28), "Sound Recording and Text Creation: Oral History and the Deliberately Concealed Garments Projects," in Maria Hayward and Elizabeth Kramer (eds.), *Textiles and Text: Re-establishing the Links between Archival and Object-based Research,* AHRC Research Centre for Textile Conservation and Textile Studies, Third Annual Conference, pp. 114–21, London: Archetype Publications.

Eco, Umberto (2007), "Social Life as a Sign System," in Malcolm Barnard (ed.), *Fashion Theory: A Reader,* pp. 143–7, London: Routledge.

Edles, Laura Desfor (2002), *Cultural Sociology in Practice,* Oxford, UK: Blackwell Publishers.

Edmunds, Holly (1999), *Focus Group Research Handbook,* New York: McGraw-Hill.

Eicher, Joanne B. (1969), *African Dress: A Selected and Annotated Bibliography of Subsaharan Countries,* Lansing, MI: African Studies Center, Michigan State University.

Eicher, Joanne B. (1976), *Nigerian Handcrafted Textiles,* Ile-Ife, Nigeria: University of Ife Press.

Eicher, Joanne B. (1998), "Beaded and Bedecked Kalabari of Nigeria," in Lidia D. Sciama and Joanne B. Eicher (eds.), *Beads and Bead Makers: Gender, Material Culture and Meaning,* pp. 95–116, Oxford, UK: Berg.

Eicher, Joanne B. (ed.) (1999), *Dress and Ethnicity: Change across Space and Time,* Oxford, UK: Berg.

Eicher, Joanne B., Sandra Lee Evenson, and Hazel A. Lutz (eds.) (2008), *The Visible Self: Global Perspectives on Dress, Culture, and Society,* New York: Fairchild Publications.

Eicher, Joanne B., and Mary Ellen Roach (eds.) (1965), *Dress, Adornment, and the Social Order,* New York: Wiley.

Eicher, Joanne B., and Mary Ellen Roach-Higgins (1992), "Definition and Classification of Dress: Implications for Analysis of Gender Roles," in Ruth Barnes and Joanne B. Eicher (eds.), *Dress and Gender: Making and Meaning in Cultural Context,* pp. 8–29, Oxford, UK: Berg.

Ellen, R. F. (ed.) (1986), *Ethnographic Research: A Guide to General Conduct (Research Methods in Social Anthropology),* London: Academic Press.

Elliot, R.E.A. (1994), "Towards a Material History Methodology," in S. Pearce (ed.), *Interpreting Objects and Collections,* pp. 109–24, London and New York: Routledge.

Engel, Laura (2009), "The Muff Affair: Fashioning Celebrity in the Portraits of Late-eighteenth-century British Actresses," in Valerie Steele (ed.), *Fashion Theory: The Journal of Dress, Body and Culture,* 13/3: 279–98, Oxford, UK: Berg.

Entwistle, Joanne (2006, September), "The Cultural Economy of Fashion Buying," in Patrik Aspers and Lise Skov (eds.), *Current Sociology,* 54/5: 704–24, Thousand Oaks, CA: Sage Publications.

Entwistle, Joanne (2009), *The Aesthetic Economy of Fashion,* Oxford, UK: Berg.

Feagin, Joe R., Anthony M. Orum, and Gideon Sjoberg (eds.) (2001), *The Case for the Case Study,* Chapel Hill: University of North Carolina Press.

Finkelstein, Joanne (1996), *After a Fashion,* Carlton, Australia: Melbourne University Press.

Finkelstein, Joanne (1999), "Chic—A Look That's Hard to See," in Valerie Steele (ed.), *Fashion Theory: The Journal of Dress, Body and Culture,* 3/3: 363–86, Oxford, UK: Berg.

Flick, Uwe (1998), *An Introduction to Qualitative Research,* Newbury Park, CA: Sage Publications.

Flugel, J. C. (1930), *The Psychology of Clothes,* London: Hogarth.

Flynn, July, Zaccagnini, Judy, and Irene M. Foster (2009), *Research Methods for the Fashion Industry,* New York: Fairchild Publications.

Fowler, Floyd J. (2002), *Survey Research Methods* (3rd edn), Applied Social Research Methods Series, Vol. 1, Thousand Oaks, CA: Sage Publications.

Garfinkel, Harold (1967), *Studies in Ethnomethodology,* Malden, MA: Polity Press/Blackwell Publishing.

Geertz, Clifford (1973), *The Interpretation of Cultures,* New York: Basic Books.

Geertz, Clifford, and George Marcus (1986), *Writing Culture: The Poetics and Politics of Ethnography,* Berkeley: University of California Press.

Giddens, Anthony (1991), *Introduction to Sociology,* New York: Norton.

Goffman, Erving (1959), *The Presentation of Self in Everyday Life,* New York: Doubleday Anchor.

Goffman, Erving (1979), *Gender Advertisements,* London: Macmillan.

Goldenberg, Phyllis (2004), *Writing a Research Paper: A Step-by-Step Approach,* New York: William H. Sadlier.

Gurova, Olga (2008), "The Art of Dressing: Body, Gender, and Discourse on Fashion in Soviet Russia 1950s–1960s," in Eugenia Paulicelli and Hazel Clark (eds.), *The Fabric of Cultures: Fashion, Identity, Globalization,* pp. 73–91, London: Routledge.

Guy, A., Green, E., and Banim, M. (eds.) (2001), *Through the Wardrobe: Women's Relationship with Their Clothes,* Oxford, UK: Berg.

Hakim, Catherine (1982), *Secondary Analysis in Social Research,* Boston: Unwin Hyman.

Hamilton, Jean A., and Hamilton, James W. (2008), "Dress as a Reflection and Sustainer of Social Reality: A Cross-cultural Perspective," in Joanne B. Eicher, Sandra Lee Evenson, and Hazel A. Lutz (eds.), *The Visible Self: Global Perspectives on Dress, Culture, and Society,* pp. 141–9, New York: Fairchild Publications.

Handley, Fiona J. L. (2005), "'I Have Bought Cloth for You and Will Deliver It Myself': Using Documentary Sources in the Analysis of the Archaeological Textile Finds from Quseir al-Qadim, Egypt," in Maria Hayward and Elizabeth Kramer (eds.), *Textiles and Text: Re-establishing the Links between Archival and Object-based Research,* pp. 10–17, London: Archetype Publications.

Hansen, Karen Tranberg (2000), *Salaula: The World of Secondhand Clothing and Zambia,* Chicago: University of Chicago Press.

Hansen, Karen Tranberg (2004), "The World in Dress: Anthropological Perspectives on Clothing Fashion and Culture," *Annual Review of Anthropology,* 33: 369–92.

Harnack, Andrew, Eugene Kleppinger, and Gene Kleppinger (2001), *Online!: A Reference Guide to Using Internet Sources,* New York: Bedford/St. Martin's.

Harni, E. J. (1932), "Pleasure in Disguise: The Need for Decoration and the Sense of Beauty," *Psychoanalytic Quarterly,* 1: 216–64.

Harper, Catherine, and Doran Ross (eds.) (2003–), *Textile: The Journal of Cloth and Culture,* Oxford, UK: Berg.

Hartzell, Preyja (2009), "The Velvet Touch: Fashion, Furniture, and the Fabric of the Interior," in Valerie Steele (ed.), *Fashion Theory: The Journal of Dress, Body and Culture,* 13/1: 51–82, Oxford, UK: Berg.

Harvey, John (1995), *Men in Black,* London: Reaktion.

Haye, Amy de la (2000), "Ethnic Minimalism: A Strand of 1990s British Fashion Identity Explored via a Contextual Analysis of Designs by Shirin Guild," in Nicola White and Ian Griffiths (eds.), *The Fashion Business: Theory, Practice, Image,* pp. 55–66, Oxford, UK: Berg.

Hayward, Maria, and Elizabeth Kramer (eds.) (2005), *Textiles and Text: Re-establishing the Links between Archival and Object-based Research,* London: Archetype Publications.

Heller, Sarah Grace (2007), *Fashion in Medieval France,* Cambridge, UK: D. S. Brewer.

Hersch, Matthew H. (2009), "Undergarment Industry and the Foundations of American Spaceflight," in Valerie Steele (ed.), *Fashion Theory: The Journal of Dress, Body and Culture,* 13/3: 345–70, Oxford, UK: Berg.

Hiler, Hilaire (1930), *From Nudity to Raiment,* London: W. and G. Foyle.

Hodkinson, Paul (2002), *Goth: Identity, Style and Subculture,* Oxford, UK: Berg.

Hollander, Anne (1993), *Seeing through Clothes,* Berkeley: University of California Press.

Hollander, Anne (1994), *Sex and Suits,* New York: Alfred A. Kopf.

Hollander, Anne (2000), *Feeding the Eye,* New York: Farrar, Straus and Giroux.

Hollander, Anne (2001), *Fabric of Vision: Dress and Drapery in Painting,* New Haven, CT: Yale University Press.

Horn, Marilyn J. (1968), *The Second Skin,* Boston: Houghton Mifflin.

Horwood, Catherine (2002), "Dressing like a Champion: Women's Tennis Wear in Interwar England," in Christopher Breward, Becky Conekin, and Caroline Cox (eds.), *The Englishness of English Dress,* pp. 45–60, Oxford, UK: Berg.

Janowski, Monica (1998), "Beads, Prestige and Life among the Kelabit of Sarawak, East Malaysia," in Lidia D. Sciama and Joanne B. Eicher (eds.), *Beads and Bead Makers: Gender, Material Culture and Meaning,* pp. 213–46, Oxford, UK: Berg.

Jasper, Cynthia, and Mary Ellen Roach-Higgins (1987), "History of Costume: Theory and Instruction," *Clothing and Textile Research Journal,* 5/4: 1–6.

Javis, Anthea (1998), "Letter from the Editor," in Anthea Javis (ed.), Special Issue: Methodology, *Fashion Theory: The Journal of Dress, Body and Culture,* 2/4: 299–300, Oxford, UK: Berg.

Johnson, Kim K. P., Susan J. Torntore, and Joanne B. Eicher (2003), *Fashion Foundations: Early Writings on Fashion and Dress,* Oxford, UK: Berg.

Jopling, Paul (2002), "On the Turn—Millennial Bodies of Time in Andrea Giacobbe's Fashion Photography," in Carol Tulloch (ed.), Special Issue: Fashion and Photography, *Fashion Theory: The Journal of Dress, Body and Culture,* 6/1: 3–24, Oxford, UK: Berg.

Kaiser, Susan B. (1998), *The Social Psychology of Clothing: Symbolic Appearances in Context,* New York: Fairchild Publications.

Kawamura, Yuniya (2004), *The Japanese Revolution in Paris Fashion,* Oxford, UK: Berg.

Kawamura, Yuniya (2005), *Fashion-ology: An Introduction to Fashion Studies,* Oxford, UK: Berg.

Kawamura, Yuniya (2006, September), "Japanese Teens as Producers of Street Fashion," in Patrik Aspers and Lise Skov (eds.), *Current Sociology,* 54/5: 784–801, Thousand Oaks, CA: Sage Publications.

Kawamura, Yuniya (2007), "Japanese Designers in Postmodern Times," in Ian Luna (ed.), *Tokyolife,* pp. 140–43, New York: Rizzoli.

Kiecolt, K. Jill, and Laura E. Nathan (1985), *Secondary Analysis of Survey Data,* Quantitative Applications in the Social Sciences Series, Beverly Hills, CA: Sage Publications.

Kinsella, Sharon (2002), "What's behind the Fetishism of Japanese School Uniforms?," in Valerie Steele (ed.), *Fashion Theory: The Journal of Dress, Body and Culture,* 6/2: 117–44, Oxford, UK: Berg.

Kirke, Betty (1998), *Madeleine Vionnet,* San Francisco: Chronicle Books.

Ko, Dorothy (1994), *Teachers of the Inner Chambers: Women and Culture in Seventeenth Century China,* Stanford, CA: Stanford University Press.

Ko, Dorothy (1997), "Bondage in Time: Footbinding and Fashion Theory," in Valerie Steele (ed.), *Fashion Theory: The Journal of Dress, Body and Culture,* 1/1: 3–27, Oxford, UK: Berg.

Ko, Dorothy (1999), "Jazzing into Modernity: High Heels, Platforms, and Lotus Shoes," in Valerie Steele and John Major (eds.), *China Chic: East Meets West*, pp. 141–53, New Haven, CT: Yale University Press.

Ko, Dorothy (2007), *Cinderella's Sisters: A Revisionist History of Foot-Binding*, Berkeley: University of California Press.

Koda, Harold (2004a), *Extreme Beauty: The Body Transformed*, New York: Metropolitan Museum of Art.

Koda, Harold (2004b), *Goddess: The Classical Mode, The Influence of Ancient Graeco-Roman Dress*, New York: Metropolitan Museum of Art.

Koda, Harold, and Andrew Bolton (2005), *Chanel*, New York: Metropolitan Museum of Art.

Koda, Harold, and Richard Martin (1993), *Diana Vreeland: Immoderate Style*, New York: Metropolitan Museum of Art.

Koda, Harold, and Richard Martin (1995a), *Haute Couture*, New York: Metropolitan Museum of Art.

Koda, Harold, and Richard Martin (1995b), *Orientalism: Visions of the East in Western Dress*, New York: Metropolitan Museum of Art.

Koda, Harold, and Richard Martin (1996), *Christian Dior*, New York: Metropolitan Museum of Art.

Kramer, Elizabeth (2005), "Introduction," in Maria Hayward and Elizabeth Kramer (eds.), *Textiles and Text: Re-establishing the Links between Archival and Object-based Research*, pp. xi–xv, London: Archetype Publications.

Kraus-Wahl, Antje (2009), "Between Studio and Catwalk—Artists in Fashion Magazines," in Valerie Steele (ed.), *Fashion Theory: The Journal of Dress, Body and Culture*, 13/1: 7–28, Oxford, UK: Berg.

Kroeber, Alfred L. (1919), "On the Principles of Order in Civilization as Exemplified by Changes of Fashion," *The American Anthropologist*, 21: 235–63.

Kroeber, Alfred L., and Jane Richardson (1940), *Three Centuries of Women's Dress Fashion: A Quantitative Analysis*, Berkeley: University of California Press.

Lane, Eliesh O'Neil (2009), *Institutional Review Boards: Decision-making in Human Subject Research*, Saarbrücken, Germany: VDM Verlag.

Lather, P. (1986), "Research as Praxis," *Harvard Educational Review*, No. 56: 257–77.

Laver, James (1995 [1969]), *Concise History of Costume and Fashion*, New York: H. N. Abrams.

Lazarsfeld, Paul F., and Rosenberg, Morris (1957), *The Language of Social Research: A Reader in the Methodology of Social Research*, Glencoe, IL: Free Press Publishers.

Lehmann, Ulrich (2000), "Language of the PurSuit: Cary Grant's Clothes in Alfred Hitchcock's 'North by Northwest,'" in Christopher Breward (ed.), Masculinities: Special Issue, *Fashion Theory: The Journal of Dress, Body and Culture*, 4/4: 476–85, Oxford, UK: Berg.

Lehmann, Ulrich (2002), *Tigersprung: Fashion in Modernity*, Cambridge, MA: MIT Press.

Leshkowich, Ann Marie (2008), "Fashioning Appropriate Youth in 1990s Vietnam," in Eugenia Paulicelli and Hazel Clark (eds.), *The Fabric of Cultures: Fashion, Identity, Globalization*, pp. 92–111, London: Routledge.

Lester, Jim D., and James D. Lester (2006), *Writing Research Papers in the Social Sciences*, Englewood Cliffs, NJ: Longman.

Lester, Jim D., and James D. Lester (2009), *Writing Research Papers*, Englewood Cliffs, NJ: Longman.

Lillethun, Abby (2007), "Introduction," in Linda Welters and Abby Lillethun (eds.), *The Fashion Reader*, pp. 77–82, Oxford, UK: Berg.

Lipovetsky, Gilles (1994), *The Empire of Fashion*, trans. Catherine Porter, Princeton, NJ: Princeton University Press.

Lomas, C. (2000), "'I Know Nothing about Fashion. There's No Point in Interviewing Me': The Use and Value of Oral History to the Fashion Historian," in S. Bruzzi and P. Church-Gibson (eds.), *Fashion Cultures: Theories, Explorations and Analysis*, pp. 363–70, London: Routledge.

Loreck, Hanne (2002), "De/constructing Fashion/Fashions of Deconstruction: Cindy Sherman's Fashion Photographs," in Valerie Steele (ed.), *Fashion Theory: The Journal of Dress, Body and Culture*, 6/3: 255–76, Oxford, UK: Berg.

Lurie, Alison (2000 [1981]), *The Language of Clothes*, New York: An Owl Book/Henry Holt.

Lyotard, Jean-François (1984), *The Postmodern Condition*, Minneapolis: University of Minnesota Press.

Mackrell, Alice (2005), *Art and Fashion: The Impact of Art on Fashion and Fashion on Art*, London: Chrysalis Books Group.

Malinowski, Bronislaw (2008 [1922]), *Argonauts of the Western Pacific: An Account of Native Enterprise and Adventure in the Archipelagoes of Melanesian New Guinea*, Whitefish, MT: Kessinger Publishing.

Maner, Martin (1999), *The Research Process: A Complete Guide and Reference for Writers*, New York: McGraw-Hill.

Manlow, Veronica (2007), *Designing Clothes: Culture and Organization of the Fashion Industry*, New Brunswick, NJ: Transaction Publishers.

Marshall, Catherine, and Gretchen B. Rossman (1999), *Designing Qualitative Research*, Newbury Park, CA: Sage Publications.

McClellan, Elizabeth (1969), *History of American Costume 1607–1800*, Clovis, CA: Tud.

McRobbie, Angela (1998), *British Fashion Design—Rag Trade or Image Industry*, London: Routledge.

Meisch, Lynn A. (1998), "'Why Do They Like Red?' Beads, Ethnicity and Gender in Ecuador," in Lidia D. Sciama and Joanne B. Eicher (eds.), *Beads and Bead Makers: Gender, Material Culture and Meaning*, pp. 147–75, Oxford, UK: Berg.

Mikhaila, Ninya, and Jane Malcolm-Davies (2005), "What Essex Man Wore: An Investigation into Elizabethan Dress Recorded in Wills 1558–1603," in Maria Hayward and Elizabeth Kramer (eds.), *Textiles and Text: Re-establishing the Links between Archival and Object-based Research*, pp. 18–22, London: Archetype Publications.

Miller, Daniel (1987), *Material Culture and Mass Consumption*, New York: Basil Blackwell.

Miller, Daniel (2005), "Introduction," in Susanne Kuchler and Daniel Miller (eds.), *Clothing as Material Culture*, pp. 1–19, Oxford, UK: Berg.

Mills, C. Wright (2000 [1959]), *The Sociological Imagination*, Oxford, UK: Oxford University Press.

Moeran, Brian (2006, September), "More Than Just a Fashion Magazine," in Patrik Aspers and Lise Skov (eds.), *Current Sociology*, 54/5: 725–44, Thousand Oaks, CA: Sage Publications.

Montesquieu, Charles de Secondat (1973 [1721]), *Persian Letters*, trans. C. J. Betts, London: Penguin Books.

Moore, Doris Langley (1949), *The Woman in Fashion*, London: Batsford.

Muggleton, David (2000), *Inside Subculture: The Postmodern Meaning of Style*, Oxford, UK: Berg.

Negrin, Llewellyn (2008), *Appearance and Identity: Fashioning the Body in Postmodernity*, New York: Palgrave Macmillan.

Neuman, W. Lawrence (2000), *Social Research Methods: Qualitative and Quantitative Approaches* (4th edn), Boston: Allyn and Bacon.

Niessen, Sandra, and Anne Brydon (1998), "Introduction: Adorning the Body," in Sandra Niessen and Anne Brydon (eds.), *Consuming Fashion: Adorning the Transnational Body*, pp. ix–xvii, Oxford, UK: Berg.

O'Connor, Kaori (2005), "The Other Half: The Material Culture of New Fibres," in Susanne Küchler and Daniel Miller (eds.), *Clothing as Material Culture,* pp. 41–60, Oxford, UK: Berg.

Olson, Kelly (2002), "Matrona and Whore: The Clothing of Women in Roman Antiquity," in Valerie Steele (ed.), *Fashion Theory: The Journal of Dress, Body and Culture,* 6/4: 387–420, Oxford, UK: Berg.

Palmer, Alexandra (1997), "New Directions: Fashion History Studies and Research in North America and England," in Valerie Steele (ed.), *Fashion Theory: The Journal of Dress, Body and Culture,* 1/3: 297–312, Oxford, UK: Berg.

Palmer, Alexandra (2001), *Couture and Commerce: Transatlantic Fashion Trade in the 1950s,* Vancouver: University of British Columbia Press.

Paulicelli, Eugenia (2004), *Fashion under Fascism: Beyond the Black Shirt,* Oxford, UK: Berg.

Paulicelli, Eugenia (2008), "Framing the Self, Staging Identity: Clothing and Italian Style in the Films of Michelagelo Antonioni (1950–1964)," in Eugenia Paulicelli and Hazel Clark (eds.), *The Fabric of Cultures: Fashion, Identity, Globalization,* pp. 53–72, London: Routledge.

Paulicelli, Eugenia, and Hazel Clark (eds.) (2008), *The Fabric of Cultures: Fashion, Identity, Globalization,* London: Routledge.

Pearce, Susan (1992), *Museum Objects and Collections,* London: Continuum International Publishing.

Pedersen, Elaine L., Sandra S. Buckland, and Christina Bates (2008–2009), "Theory and Dress Scholarship: A Discussion on Developing and Applying Theory," *Dress: The Annual Journal of the Costume Society of America,* 35: 71–85.

Perrot, Philippe (1994), *Fashioning the Bourgeoisie: A History of Clothing in the Nineteenth Century,* trans. Richard Bienvenu, Princeton, NJ: Princeton University Press.

Prown, Jules (1982), "Mind in Matter: An Introduction to Material Culture Theory and Method," *Winterthur Portfolio,* 17/2: 1–17.

Quicherat, J. (1877), *Histoire du costume en France depuis les temps les plus reculés juau'a la fin de XVIII siècle,* Paris: Librairie Hachette et Cie.

Quinn, Bradley (2002), "A Note: Hussein Chalayan, Fashion and Technology," in Valerie Steele (ed.), *Fashion Theory: The Journal of Dress, Body and Culture,* 6/4: 359–68, Oxford, UK: Berg.

Racinet, Albert Charles (1888), *Le costume historique,* Paris: firmin-Didot.

Radcliffe-Brown, Sir A. R. (1922), *The Andaman Islanders,* Cambridge, UK: Cambridge University Press.

Rantisi, Norma (2006), "How New York Stole Modern Fashion," in Christopher Breward and David Gilbert (eds.), *Fashion's World Cities,* pp. 109–22, Oxford, UK: Berg.

Rea, Louis M., and Richard A. Parker (2005), *Designing and Conducting Survey Research: A Comprehensive Guide,* Hoboken, NJ: Jossey-Bass.

Remaury, Bruno (ed.) (1996), *Dictionnaire de la mode au XXe siècle,* Paris: Editions du Regard.

Rexford, Nancy (1988), "Studying Garments for Their Own Sake: Mapping the World of Costume Scholarship," *Dress,* 14: 68–75.

Ribeiro, Aileen (1995), *The Art of Dress: Fashion in England and France 1750 to 1820,* New Haven, CT: Yale University Press.

Ribeiro, Aileen (1998), "Re-fashioning Art: Some Visual Approaches to the Study of the History of Dress," in Anthea Javis (ed.), Special Issue: Methodology, *Fashion Theory: The Journal of Dress, Body and Culture,* 2/4: 315–26, Oxford, UK: Berg.

Roach, Mary Ellen, and Joanne B. Eicher (eds.) (1965), *Dress, Adornment and Social Order,* New York: Wiley.

Roach-Higgins, Mary, and Joanne Eicher (1973), *The Visible Self: Perspectives on Dress,* Englewood Cliffs, NJ: Prentice-Hall.

Rocamora, Agnès (2001, June), "High Fashion and Pop Fashion: The Symbolic Production of Fashion in *Le Monde* and *The Guardian,*" in Valerie Steele (ed.), *Fashion Theory: The Journal of Dress, Body and Culture,* 5/2: 123–42, Oxford, UK: Berg.

Roche, Daniel (1994), *The Culture of Clothing: Dress and Fashion in the Ancien Regime,* trans. Jean Birrell, Cambridge, UK: Cambridge University Press.

Rose, Clare (2005), "Bought, Stolen, Bequeathed, Preserved: Sources for the Study of 18th-century Petticoats," in Maria Hayward and Elizabeth Kramer (eds.), *Textiles and Text: Reestablishing the Links between Archival and Object-based Research,* pp. 114–21, London: Archetype Publications.

Rosencranz, Mary Lou (1965), *Clothing Concepts: A Social-psychological Approach,* New York: Macmillan.

Rousseau, Jean-Jacques (1997 [1750]), *Discours sur les sciences et les arts,* Paris: Gallimard.

Ryan, Mary Shaw (1966), *Clothing: A Study in Human Behavior,* New York: Holt, Rinehart & Winston.

Sapir, Edward (1931), "Fashion," *Encyclopedia of the Social Sciences,* Vol. 6, pp. 139–44, London: Macmillan.

Saussure, Ferdinand de (1966 [1916]), *Course in General Linguistics,* translator unknown, New York: McGraw-Hill.

Sciama, Lidia D., and Eicher, Joanne B. (eds.) (1998), *Beads and Bead Makers: Gender, Material Culture and Meaning,* Oxford, UK: Berg.

Shin, Kristine (ed.) (2008–), *The International Journal of Fashion Design, Technology and Education,* London: Francis and Taylor.

Shukla, Pravina (2007), *The Grace of Four Moons: Dress, Adornment and the Art of Body in Modern India,* Bloomington: Indiana University Press.

Simmel, Georg (1957, May [1904]), "Fashion," *American Journal of Sociology,* 62/6: 541–58.

Skjold, Else (2008), "Fashion Research at Design Schools," unpublished PhD dissertation, Designskolen Kolding, Jutland, Sweden.

Skov, Lise (1996, August), "Fashion Trends, Japonisme and Postmodernism," *Theory, Culture and Society,* 13/3: 129–51.

Skov, Lise (2006, September), "The Role of Trade Fairs in the Global Fashion Business," in Patrik Aspers and Lise Skov (eds.), *Current Sociology,* 54/5: 765–83, Thousand Oaks, CA: Sage Publications.

Sokolowski, Robert (1999), *Introduction to Phenomenology,* Cambridge, UK: Cambridge University Press.

Söll, Änne (2009), "Pollock in Vogue: American Fashion and Avant-garde Art in Cecil Beaton's 1951 Photographs," in Valerie Steele (ed.), *Fashion Theory: The Journal of Dress, Body and Culture,* 13/1: 29–50, Oxford, UK: Berg.

Spooner, Catherine (2004), *Fashioning Gothic Bodies,* Manchester, UK: Manchester University Press.

Stebbins, Robert Alan (2001), *Exploratory Research in the Social Sciences (Qualitative Research Methods),* London: Sage Publications.

Steele, Valerie (1985), *Fashion and Eroticism: Ideals of Feminine Beauty from the Victorian Era through the Jazz Age,* New York: Oxford University Press.

Steele, Valerie (1988), *Paris Fashion: A Cultural History,* New York: Oxford University Press.

Steele, Valerie (1991), *Women of Fashion: Twentieth Century Designers,* New York: Rizzoli.

Steele, Valerie (1998), "A Museum of Fashion Is More Than a Clothes-Bag," in Anthea Javis (ed.), Special Issue: Methodology, *Fashion Theory: The Journal of Dress, Body and Culture*, 2/4: 327–36, Oxford, UK: Berg.

Steele, Valerie (2000), "Fashion: Yesterday, Today and Tomorrow," in Nicola White and Ian Griffiths (eds.), *The Fashion Business: Theory, Practice, Image*, pp. 7–20, Oxford, UK: Berg.

Steele, Valerie (2003), *The Corset: A Cultural History*, New Haven, CT: Yale University Press.

Steele, Valerie (ed.) (1997–), *Fashion Theory: The Journal of Dress, Body and Culture*, Oxford, UK: Berg.

Steele, Valerie, and John Major (eds.) (1999), *China Chic: East Meets West*, New Haven, CT: Yale University Press.

Stokes, Jane C. (2003), *How to Do Media and Cultural Studies*, London: Sage Publications.

Stone, Gregory (1962), "Appearance and the Self," in Arnold Rose (ed.), *Human Behavior and Social Processes*, pp. 86–118, Boston: Houghton Mifflin.

Styles, John (1998), "Dress in History: Reflections on a Contested Terrain," in Anthea Javis (ed.), Special Issue: Methodology, *Fashion Theory: The Journal of Dress, Body and Culture*, 2/4: 383–9, Oxford, UK: Berg.

Summers, Leigh (2001), *Bound to Please: A History of the Victorian Corset*, Oxford, UK: Berg.

Sumner, William Graham (1940 [1906]), *Folkways: A Study of the Sociological Importance of Usages, Manners, Customs, Mores and Morals*, Boston: Ginn and Company.

Tarde, Gabriel (1903), *The Laws of Imitation*, trans. Elsie C. Parsons, New York: Henry Holt.

Tarlo, Emma (1996), *Clothing Matters: Dress and Identity in India*, Chicago: University of Chicago Press.

Tarlo, Emma (2010), *Visibly Muslim: Fashion, Politics, Faith*, Oxford, UK: Berg.

Taylor, George R. (ed.) (2005), *Integrating Quantitative and Qualitative Methods in Research* (2nd edn), Lanham, MD: University Press of America.

Taylor, Lou (1998), "Doing the Laundry: A Reassessment of Object-based Dress History," in Valerie Steele (ed.), *Fashion Theory: The Journal of Dress, Body and Culture*, 2/4: 337–58, Oxford, UK: Berg.

Taylor, Lou (2000), "The Hilfiger Factor and the Flexible Commercial World of Couture," in Nicola White and Ian Griffiths (eds.), *The Fashion Business: Theory, Practice, Image*, pp. 121–42, Oxford, UK: Berg.

Taylor, Lou (2002a), *The Study of Dress History*, Manchester, UK: Manchester University Press.

Taylor, Lou (2002b), "Why the Absence of Fashionable Dress in the Victoria and Albert Museum's Exhibition Art Nouveau, 1890–1914?," in Valerie Steele (ed.), *Fashion Theory: The Journal of Dress, Body and Culture*, 6/3: 311–22, Oxford, UK: Berg.

Taylor, Lou (2004), *Establishing Dress History*, Manchester, UK: Manchester University Press.

Theatre de la Mode, The (1991), Documentary Video, Telos Production.

Thibaul, Paul J. (1997), *Re-reading Saussure: The Dynamics of Signs in Social Life*, London and New York: Routledge.

Thompson, Steven K. (2002), *Sampling*, Hoboken, NJ: Wiley-Interscience.

Toennies, Ferdinand (1961 [1909]), *Custom: An Essay on Social Codes*, trans. A. F. Borenstein, New York: Free Press.

Tortora, Phyllis G., and Keith Eubank (2009), *Survey of Historic Costume*, New York: Fairchild Publications.

Troy, Nancy J. (2002), "Paul Poiret's Minaret Style: Originality, Reproduction, and Art in Fashion," in Valerie Steele (ed.), *Fashion Theory: The Journal of Dress, Body and Culture*, 6/2: 117–44, Oxford, UK: Berg.

Trumbull, Michael (2005), "Qualitative Research Methods," in George R. Taylor (ed.), *Integrating of Quantitative and Qualitative Methods in Research,* pp. 101–26, Lanham, MD: University Press of America.

Tseëlon, Efrat (1994), "Fashion and Signification in Baudrillard," in Douglas Kellner (ed.), *Baudrillard: A Critical Reader,* pp. 119–32, Oxford, UK: Basil Blackwell.

Tseëlon, Efrat (2001), "Fashion Research and Its Discontents," in Valerie Steele (ed.), *Fashion Theory: The Journal of Dress, Body and Culture,* 5/4: 435–52, Oxford, UK: Berg.

Tseëlon, Efrat, Ana Marta González, and Susan Kaiser (eds.) (2010–), *Critical Studies in Fashion and Beauty,* Bristol, UK: Intellect.

Tu, Rachel (2008), "Dressing the Nation: Indian Cinema Costume and the Making of a National Fashion 1947–1957," in Eugenia Paulicelli and Hazel Clark (eds.), *The Fabric of Cultures: Fashion, Identity, Globalization,* pp. 12–27, London: Routledge.

Tulloch, Carol (1998), "Out of Many, One People: The Relativity of Dress, Race and Ethnicity to Jamaica, 1880–1907," in Anthea Javis (ed.), Special Issue: Methodology, *Fashion Theory: The Journal of Dress, Body and Culture,* 2/4: 359–80, Oxford, UK: Berg.

Tulloch, Carol (ed.) (2002), "Special Issue: Fashion and Photography," *Fashion Theory: The Journal of Dress, Body and Culture,* 6/1, Oxford, UK: Berg.

Turney, Jo (2005), "(Ad)Dressing the Century: Fashionability and Floral Frocks," in Maria Hayward and Elizabeth Kramer (eds.), *Textiles and Text: Re-establishing the Links between Archival and Object-based Research,* pp. 58–64, London: Archetype Publications.

Veblen, Thornstein (1957 [1899]), *The Theory of Leisure Class,* London: Allen and Unwin.

Weber, Max (1949), *The Methodology of the Social Sciences,* New York: Free Press.

Weber, Max (1968), *Economy and Society—An Outline of Interpretative Sociology,* New York: Bedminster Press.

Weber, Max (1970), "Class, Status, Party," in H. H. Gerth and C. W. Mills (eds.), *From Max Weber: Essays in Sociology,* pp. 180–95, London: Routledge and Kegan Paul.

Weber, Max (1978 [1909]), *Economy & Society,* Vol. 1, edited by Guenther Roth and Claus Wittich, Berkeley: University of California Press.

Welters, Linda, and Patricia A. Cunningham (2005), *Twentieth Century American Fashion,* Oxford, UK: Berg.

Welters, Linda, and Abby Lillethun (eds.), *The Fashion Reader,* Oxford, UK: Berg.

Whitaker, Maureen (2007, May), "Fashion History: A Case Study in Multidisciplinary and Comparative Methodologies," unpublished MA thesis, Fashion and Textile Studies: History, Theory and Museum Practice, the Fashion Institute of Technology.

White, Nicola, and Ian Griffiths (2000a), "Introduction: The Fashion Business Theory, Practice, Image," in Nicola White and Ian Griffiths (eds.), *The Fashion Business: Theory, Practice, Image,* pp. 1–4, Oxford, UK: Berg.

White, Nicola, and Ian Griffiths (eds.) (2000b), *The Fashion Business: Theory, Practice, Image,* Oxford, UK: Berg.

Wilkie, Laurie A. (1998), "Beads and Breasts: The Negotiation of Gender Roles and Power at New Orleans *Mardi Gras,*" in Lidia D. Sciama and Joanne B. Eicher (eds.), *Beads and Bead Makers: Gender, Material Culture and Meaning,* pp. 193–211, Oxford, UK: Berg.

Williamson, Judith (1978), *Decoding Advertisements: Ideology and Meaning in Advertising,* London: Boyars.

Wilson, Elizabeth (1985), *Adorned in Dreams: Fashion and Modernity,* Berkeley: University of California Press.

Woodward, Sophie (2009), "The Myth of Street Style," in Valerie Steele (ed.), *Fashion Theory: The Journal of Dress, Body and Culture,* 13/1: 83–102, Oxford, UK: Berg.

Worth, Rachel (1999), "Rural Laboring Dress, 1850–1900: Some Problems of Representation," in Valerie Steele (ed.), *Fashion Theory: The Journal of Dress, Body and Culture*, 3/3:
  323–42, Oxford, UK: Berg.
Yagou, Artemis (2009), "On Apes and Aping: Fashion Modernity and Evolutionary Theories
  in Nineteenth-century Greece," in Valerie Steele (ed.), *Fashion Theory: The Journal of
  Dress, Body and Culture*, 13/3: 325–44, Oxford, UK: Berg.
Young, Agnes B. (1937), *Recurring Cycles of Fashion*, New York: Harper and Brothers.

INDEX

9 781847 885821